Praise f

eating pu___ ___,

"I love the philosophy of Elizabeth's Eating Purely Principles, which make healthy eating accessible to all. The recipes in the cookbook are easy to prepare, creative, and totally delicious . . . plus, they are purely healthy."

—Bobbi Brown, COO, **Bobbi Brown Cosmetics**

"Elizabeth's cookbook is a beautiful reflection of her healthy and delicious products. If more people started eating purely, the world would be in a much better place. We are so proud that she's a graduate of our Health Coach Training Program!"

—Joshua Rosenthal, **founder, director, and primary teacher, Institute for Integrative Nutrition**

"Elizabeth created the first gluten-free, superfood-packed, commercially distributed granola that doesn't compromise taste. But it's not just about food, and if anyone gets it, it's Elizabeth. It's about going for your dreams, being gentle with yourself, moving with ease, and eating whole foods. Eating Purely is a treasure chest of pure, creative recipes and healthy pantry tips that everyone in your family will love!"

—Ksenia Avdulova, **founder and chief superfoodie, Breakfast Criminals**

eating purely.

eating purely.

100 all-natural, organic,
gluten-free recipes for a healthy life

Written and Photographed by
Elizabeth Stein

Foreword by Bobbi Brown

Skyhorse Publishing

Copyright © 2015 by Elizabeth Stein
Foreword copyright © by Bobbi Brown
Photographs copyright © 2015 by Elizabeth Stein
First Skyhorse Publishing paperback edition, 2021.

All rights reserved. No part of this book may be reproduced in any manner without
the express written consent of the publisher, except in the case of brief excerpts
in critical reviews or articles. All inquiries should be addressed to Skyhorse
Publishing, 307 West 36th Street, 11th Floor, New York, NY 10018.

Skyhorse Publishing books may be purchased in bulk at special discounts for
sales promotion, corporate gifts, fund-raising, or educational purposes. Special
editions can also be created to specifications. For details, contact the Special Sales
Department, Skyhorse Publishing, 307 West 36th Street, 11th Floor, New York, NY
10018 or info@skyhorsepublishing.com.

Skyhorse® and Skyhorse Publishing® are registered trademarks of Skyhorse
Publishing, Inc.®, a Delaware corporation.

Visit our website at www.skyhorsepublishing.com.

10 9 8 7 6 5 4 3 2 1

Library of Congress Cataloging-in-Publication Data is available on file.

Cover design by Caroline Caligari
Cover photo credit: Elizabeth Stein
Interior design by Caroline Caligari

Print ISBN: 978-1-5107-5769-1
Ebook ISBN: 978-1-5107-0060-4

Printed in China

dedicated to my mom and
dad for allowing me to go after
my wildest dreams.

table of contents

FOREWORD

By Bobbi Brown, New York

After tasting Purely Elizabeth's granola, I contacted Elizabeth to let her know how much I loved her product line. Soon after, we met for coffee in New York City and traded stories of start-ups, growing a brand, and having a product with your name on it. I casually suggested she write a cookbook and am so thrilled to see her beautiful finished work. I love the philosophy of her Eating Purely principles, which make healthy eating accessible to all. The recipes in the cookbook are easy to prepare, creative, and totally delicious . . . plus they are purely healthy.

I'm a huge fan of eating healthy—I guess you can say it's a passion of mine, and has been since I started my career. So much of my beauty philosophy has been about feeling good and taking care of your body. To this day, I continue to empower women to feel comfortable in their own skin, because when you feel good about yourself, there's no limit to what you can do. Beauty and a healthy lifestyle go hand in hand—what you put in your body is just as important as what you put on it.

While I was growing up, my mom taught me the importance of eating for nutrition, and it's something that I've passed down to my family. Eating healthy food keeps me going, and there's no denying you look great when you choose nutrient-dense foods. Diet should mean eating to live and choosing foods that taste good and do good. Water, lots of veggies, fresh juices, whole grains, fruits, lean protein, and fiber are all amazing beauty foods. When I eat right, my skin glows, my eyes are brighter, I have more energy, and my body is happy because it's healthy.

When it comes down to it, remember to keep your body (both inside and out) healthy and in good working order by nourishing it every day. After all, you only get one body, so it's important to treat it right. Your body will thank you by giving you everything you need to look and feel your best.

As a makeup artist, I'm often asked my definition of beauty. To me, it is simple. Be the happiest and healthiest version of who you are, because when you feel good, you look good. How do you achieve this? Eat purely.

INTRODUCTION

"Start a natural foods company." Those were the words I wrote down on the blank piece of paper in front of me as I sat in beautiful upstate New York in October 2007 while on a retreat with my holistic nutrition school, the Institute for Integrative Nutrition.

My instructor had just asked us to describe our "unpredictable future," and while I saw no clear path of how to get there, I knew one thing for certain: I wanted to start a company to help others eat better, feel better, and live better. One short month later, without any idea of how to start a natural foods company—where to source ingredients or how to get a product on the shelf at a local market—**Purely Elizabeth** was born.

From the start, the response was immediate and overwhelming. Within our first week of business, we received incredible press from the trend-setting site DailyCandy. Consumers clamored for our delicious, healthy mixes, and we could hardly keep up with the demand—yikes! Family and friends all joined forces, working around the clock in a commercial kitchen, mixing, measuring, and packaging products by hand. The beginning days were both crazy and incredibly exciting. I never dreamed it would all happen so quickly. We've come a long way from the days of mixing and packaging everything ourselves. Today, **Purely Elizabeth** products are distributed nationally throughout the country in thousands of retailers, including Whole Foods Markets, Target, Wegmans, and Dean & DeLuca.

Write a cookbook. That was my goal. I wrote it down on iPhone "Notes" and hoped for the best. So a month later when I got a call out of nowhere to see if I was interested in writing a cookbook, I knew it was meant to be. I've definitely learned that there is power in what you set your intentions to, and I've realized that I better be careful what I write down!

So why write this cookbook? Well, from the beginning, I'd always envisioned **Purely Elizabeth** to be more than just a natural foods company. I dreamed of creating an enduring brand and platform to educate people about health and wellness. (I am a holistic nutrition counselor after all!) **Purely Elizabeth** grew from the idea that healthy food should be delicious, never a sacrifice. Good health begins with what you put into your body. When you eat better, you feel better. It's that simple: you are what you eat. While this belief is the foundation on which our company was created, **Purely Elizabeth** has since evolved into a lifestyle brand, focused not only on providing you with the best food Mother Nature has to offer in its purest form, but also to arm you with the knowledge and tools to live the healthy, balanced, and energy-filled life you deserve!

A key reason for starting **Purely Elizabeth** was that I recognized a gap in the market for healthy gluten-free foods. At the time, 99 percent of the gluten-free products on the market were loaded with refined sugar (to cover up the icky taste!) as well as with refined flours like potato starch and white rice flour. I liked to joke that the gluten-free world of the 2000s, was like the fat-free craze of the 1990s. The products on the market may have been "gluten-free," but they were far from healthy, and still, people gobbled them up. And like the fat-free craze of the 1990s, when people consumed large quantities of low-fat and no-fat foods not realizing they were packed with sugar, calories, and little nutrition, people wondered why they didn't feel so good, why they weren't keeping the weight off, and in some cases, why they were developing diabetes. The situation was a mess. But I realized that I had an opportunity to do something better to help people live healthier lives.

So I started experimenting in my tiny Manhattan kitchen. At the time, I was just learning about the wonderful health benefits of superfood seeds—like hemp, chia, and quinoa—and started incorporating these ingredients into everything I was making. That approach has become the backbone of everything we do at **Purely Elizabeth**—and here in my first cookbook. My philosophy is to take familiar and well-loved foods and prepare them using the most nutrient-rich ingredients, which leaves you feeling more energized, healthy, and radiant. If you're going to eat a chocolate chip cookie, for example, why not throw in some chia seeds for added fiber, protein, and omega-3s? And while you're at it, why not use organic coconut sugar to replace refined sugar so that your blood sugar doesn't soar? This thinking is at the heart of everything we do at the company. It's all about making simple diet and lifestyle changes to start eating and living purely.

My philosophy of **eating purely** is centered on the following five principles: Eat Whole, Clean Foods; Focus on Plants; Add in Nutrient-Rich Ingredients; Kick Inflammatory Foods to the Curb; and Practice the 80/20 Rule. But most importantly, I believe that you never have to sacrifice taste when eating healthy foods. I love the fact that I can have friends over, cook an entirely healthy, vegetarian meal—and no one walks out the door hungry or craving something more (even the meat-and-potatoes guests!).

The recipes in **Eating Purely** will introduce you to new ways to cook and eat healthfully in an easy, fast manner that even the most novice chef can master. The dishes can be enjoyed any night of the week with family and friends. I am beyond grateful for this opportunity to share with you my favorite recipes along with nutrition tips and strategies for **eating purely** and living purely. I hope you enjoy!

Now come on, dig in!

EAT PURELY. LIVE PURELY.

Elizabeth

CHAPTER 1
EATING PURELY PRINCIPLES

The five Eating Purely Principles are:

1. Eat Whole, Clean Foods
2. Focus on Plants
3. Kick Inflammatory Foods to the Curb
4. Add in Nutrient-Rich Ingredients
5. Practice the 80/20 Rule

1. Eat Whole, Clean Foods

Whole foods are whole, meaning those with their vitamins, nutrients, and fibers still intact. Whole foods are not processed or refined in any way. It's food in its purest form, the way Mother Nature intended. Readily available for your body to use as energy to fuel your day, whole foods make you feel great! Unlike refined, processed foods, whole foods do not cause mood swings or low energy. Those switching to a whole foods–based diet often report increased energy, vitality, and happiness. Examples of whole foods include fruits and vegetables, whole grains, nuts, and seeds. When shopping for whole foods, make sure to look for the "cleaner" or organic option. Organic foods do not have added herbicides, pesticides, artificial additives, or other unknown fungicides and have not been genetically modified. Chemicals used in nonorganic foods can leave toxins in the body that ultimately make us not function optimally. For this reason, I suggest trying to incorporate as many organic foods as possible. With so many pollutants in our everyday lives, if we can control some of them, then all the better. Though organic foods can sometimes be more expensive, you are investing in your health and future well-being. The best health insurance you can have for the future is to eat well today. And really, who wants to eat foods that have been sprayed with chemicals?!

2. Focus on Plants

Plant-based foods are loaded with vitamins, minerals, and nutrients. In particular, leafy greens like kale, Swiss chard, spinach, and arugula rank high on this list. These leafy greens are high in vitamin C, calcium, magnesium, and zinc and have incredible healing proprieties that help you lose weight, gain energy, and feel fantastic. Try to incorporate leafy greens into every meal, filling half your plate with the bright plants. They will fill you up but won't fill you out! A win-win for all.

No single diet works for everyone. So I don't suggest that everyone should eliminate animal products from their diet, but I do recommend minimizing them. Why? Because studies show that eliminating animal products from your diet benefits both your health and the environment. Along with increasing your risk for a variety of diseases, including heart disease and cancer, consuming animal products can have severe negative consequences on the environment. Raising farm animals generates more global warming greenhouse gases than transportation, generates deforestation, and damages our increasingly scarce water sources.

So if it feels right to completely remove animal products from your diet—more power to you. However, if you feel better with some animal protein, go ahead and enjoy. But remember it should be in small quantities, not half of your plate and definitely organic!

3. Kick Inflammatory Foods to the Curb

Inflammation in the body is one of the top causes of disease, cellular breakdown, and weight gain. Who wants that?! To kick inflammation to the curb, decrease your consumption of inflammatory, high-stress foods. These include:

- refined sugars
- processed foods
- wheat—any gluten-containing ingredients
- bad oils/fats (such as hydrogenated oil, trans fats, oils high in omega-6s)
- excess animal protein
- dairy

Effects of these inflammatory foods include feeling congested, heavy, low in energy, moody, and having a lowered immune response—and that's just to name a few. What you put in your body is not the only thing that causes inflammation—environmental factors such as stress, lack of exercise, toxins, and free radicals do, too. So remember, get in your workouts, stop stressing, and watch for toxins!

Inflammation is part of your body's natural defense system. When your body senses natural invaders, your white blood cells mobilize to protect you. When your system is out of balance, inflammation can run rampant in your body, causing a chronic fire of inflammation leading to disease and weight gain. Those who take inflammatory foods out of their diet report having energy levels go through the roof, shedding excess weight, breathing better, and feeling lighter, stronger, and more powerful.

4. Add in Nutrient-Rich Ingredients

Nutrient-rich ingredients include those foods high in antioxidants, omega-3s, vitamins, and minerals—all of the things that your body needs to function optimally. Including these nutrients in your diet helps you to feel great, have more energy, stay healthy, and even look amazing.

OMEGA-3s:

Omega-3s make up cell membranes around the body, especially in the eyes and brain. Once omega-3s enter your cells, they help increase fat burning, improve your blood sugar control, correct insulin resistance, and reduce inflammation. Deficiencies in omega-3s have been tied to autism, attention deficit disorder, depression, Alzheimer's, and learning disabilities in children.

A major factor in having "enough" omega-3s is having a balance between omega-3 and omega-6 fatty acids. An ideal ration would be 1:1, but most Americans' diets have a much higher ratio.

Sources of omega-3 fatty acids are: fatty fish like salmon, grass-fed animal foods, walnuts, flaxseeds, hemp seeds, and chia seeds to name a few. Chia, hemp, and flax are easy to keep in your kitchen arsenal and throw on anything and everything you are eating to give your meal an added nutrient boost.

Sources of omega-6 fatty acids are: polyunsaturated vegetable oil (such as canola and safflower oil) and meats raised on grains devoid of omega-3s.

ANTIOXIDANT-RICH FOODS:

Antioxidants are crucial for our overall health because they fight off free radicals that fuel inflammation. Free radicals are highly reactive oxygen molecules that damage cells and contribute to chronic disease and overall immunity. Where do free radicals come from? They come from excessive exercise, inflammatory foods, chemicals and toxins, not enough sleep, the sun, and low levels of friendly gut bacteria. The job of antioxidants is to neutralize the oxidative stress caused by free-radical damage. Antioxidants then protect and repair damaged cells. We want to consume as many antioxidant-rich foods as possible to clean up and get those toxins out!

Antioxidant-rich foods are particularly high in vitamins A, C, and E. This includes berries (blueberries, raspberries, blackberries, and strawberries), greens (like kale, spinach, artichoke, and broccoli), legumes (black beans and kidney beans), nuts and grains (such as pecans, walnuts, quinoa, and oats).

5. Practice the 80/20 Rule

So what does that mean? Well, 80 percent of the time follow the ideas in this book and 20 percent of the time let loose (in moderation, of course). The 80/20 Rule allows you to not feel guilty for eating that slice of pizza on Saturday night. It frees you from the idea of perfection and allows you to just enjoy every moment of life, because that's what it's about, right?

A few more tips to help you feel purely wonderful . . .

1. DRINK MORE WATER—Try to drink half your body weight in ounces. Most of us are chronically dehydrated. There are so many problems that can be cleared by simply drinking more water.

2. COOK OFTEN—Cooking can be relaxing and fun and also helps us to connect with our food—where it's coming from and how it makes us feel. Cooking also saves money and, often times, calories.

3. EAT ACCORDING TO THE SEASONS—Keep your body in balance with the foods that are available seasonally. Watermelon is available in summer (to cool us down) and squashes are available in winter (to warm us up).

4. HAVE HEALTHY RELATIONSHIPS—At the end of the day, if we don't feel supported by loved ones, we are likely going to dive into that gallon of Jeni's ice cream. When we feel loved and supported, it's a lot easier to stay healthy.

5. DO PHYSICAL ACTIVITY REGULARLY—Whether you like to run, hike, bike, or do yoga, find what works for you and do it often. I find that even 20 minutes of movement in the morning changes my entire outlook for the day. To see results in your body and mind, you need to be consistent. I like to get in exercise at least five days a week.

Most importantly, remember: YOU ARE WHAT YOU EAT . . . SO EAT PURELY!

CHAPTER 2
KITCHEN STAPLES

The list on the following pages includes the must-have items for any **eating purely** pantry. These are my favorite foods and products to have on hand so I can make a healthy meal in a pinch. If you are unfamiliar with some items, hopefully this list will help clear up any confusion—and perhaps introduce you to something new and life-changing. Most items can be found in your local grocery store.

ALMOND BUTTER. Almond butter is a delicious, healthy alternative to traditional peanut butter, perfect to spread on sandwiches, include in smoothies, or utilize in sauces. Almonds are a nutritional powerhouse that contains significant amounts of protein, calcium, fiber, magnesium, folic acid, potassium, and vitamin E. **Favorite Brand: Once Again Organic Almond Butter Creamy**

ALMOND FLOUR. I love almond flour because it's not really flour; it's just ground up almonds, so since it's grain-free, it's a great option if you are sticking to a Paleo diet. Almond flour is rich in magnesium as well as vitamin E, a powerful antioxidant. **Favorite Brand: King Arthur Flour Almond Flour**

APPLE CIDER VINEGAR. Thought to be a miracle cure-all, apple cider vinegar has countless uses. I stock it in my pantry to ferment veggies, add to salad dressings, and mix with milk to create buttermilk for baked goods. See page 93 for more uses. **Favorite Brand: Bragg Organic Apple Cider Vinegar**

ARROWROOT POWDER. Native to South America, arrowroot powder is a starch that comes from the arrowroot plant. With a neutral flavor, it is often substituted for cornstarch or flour in gluten-free baking and can also be used as a thickener for sauces, jams, puddings, you name it. **Favorite Brand: Bob's Red Mill Arrowroot Starch**

BROWN RICE FLOUR. A versatile gluten-free flour, brown rice flour is nutrient-rich with a mild taste. With the bran still intact, it makes for a much healthier choice over white rice flour. Look for superfine varieties that will not leave a gritty taste. It'll be even better if you can find sprouted brown rice flour in stores. **Favorite Brand: Bob's Red Mill Brown Rice Flour**

BROWN RICE PASTA. This is my favorite traditional pasta alternative. It tastes much better than typical whole grain pastas and is also gluten-free. Be sure to look for a brand that is high in fiber such as Lundberg, my favorite. **Favorite Brand: Lundberg Family Farms Organic Brown Rice Spaghetti Pasta**

CHIA SEEDS. Chia seeds are a powerful superfood once used as currency for their exceptional value. The Aztec warriors used this endurance seed, rich in omega-3 fatty acids, fiber, and protein to run great distances. Studies show that eating chia seeds slows down how fast our bodies convert carbohydrate calories into simple sugars. Look for Salba® Chia, the most nutritionally consistent and nutrient dense form of chia on the planet. **Favorite Brand: Salba Smart Organic Raw Whole Chia Seeds**

COCONUT OIL. Coconut oil is made of lauric acid, a medium-chain fatty acid found in mother's milk that supports healthy metabolism as well as offering anti-fungal, anti-viral, and anti-bacterial properties. The medium-chain fatty acids get used as energy rather than stored as fat in the body. Unlike other fats, extra virgin coconut oil is high in medium-chain fatty acids that help you lose weight, lower cholesterol, improve diabetic conditions, and reduce the risk of heart disease. **Favorite Brand: Spectrum Unrefined Organic Virgin Coconut Oil**

COCONUT SUGAR. Coconut sugar is made from the sap or nectar of the palm tree flower. The Food and Agriculture Organization has even named this sugar the world's most sustainable sweetener. Measuring low on the glycemic index (35), it is also nutrient-rich—high in many vitamins and minerals such as potassium, magnesium, zinc, iron, and B vitamins. Coconut sugar is my favorite sweetener to use for any sugar substitute due to its taste and health properties. It's also simple to swap into any recipes as it has a 1:1 ratio to regular sugar. **Favorite Brand: Big Tree Farms Organic Coconut Sugar**

GARBANZO FAVA BEAN FLOUR. Garbanzo fava bean flour contains high levels of protein and fiber. Garbanzo bean flour is traditionally used in Middle Eastern cooking and baking. It can have a strong flavor, so I use it as a small ration in my flour blends to bake. **Favorite Brand: Bob's Red Mill Garbanzo Fava Bean Flour**

HEMP SEEDS. Hemp seeds were first used in China more than six thousand years ago as a staple food. Rich in omega-3 fatty acids and protein, hemp seeds are considered a perfect food. This superfood is also rich in sulfur, known as the beauty mineral, as well as iron and vitamin E. I love throwing hemp seeds on top of salad, soups, cereals, even pasta for added nutrition, crunch, and nutty flavor. **Favorite Brand: Manitoba Harvest Organic Hemp Hearts**

HIMALAYAN SEA SALT. Himalayan sea salt is thought to be the purest salt on Earth, containing more than eighty-four minerals that help balance the body. This is my salt of choice for all of my cooking and baking. **Favorite Brand: HimalaSalt Himalayan Sea Salt**

MILLET FLOUR. I use millet flour in a lot of my baking recipes. It carries a very mild taste and, when mixed with other flours, performs beautifully as a gluten-free flour option. Millet is an ancient grain, rich in B vitamins, which helps support metabolism, increase immunity, and enhance energy levels. Originating in North Africa, but now grown in the US, Millet is often thought of as food "for the birds." **Favorite Brand: Bob's Red Mill Millet Flour**

MIRIN. Mirin is a popular Japanese cooking wine, characterized by a sweet taste and low alcohol content. I love using the ingredient with some tamari and sesame oil for a delicious Asian sauce. **Favorite Brand: Eden Foods Mirin**

MISO. Miso is a fermented soybean paste that originated in Japan. Although miso is usually made from soybeans, it can also be produced from rice, barley, or wheat by adding a yeast mold. Be sure to look for the gluten-free variety. Miso is high in protein, b12, zinc, and trace minerals and is great for digestion and strengthening the immune system. It is also high in antioxidants. My favorite miso is the sweet white miso from Miso Master. **Favorite Brand: Miso Master Organic Mellow White Miso**

NUTRITIONAL YEAST. Yellow in color and with a nutty cheesy flavor, nutritional yeast is an inactive yeast that is a favorite amongst many vegans since it's a source of b12. Sprinkle some on popcorn, stir into pasta, or mix with cashews to create a ricotta-like cheese. **Favorite Brand: Buy from bulk section at health food store**

QUINOA. Quinoa, an ancient grain considered sacred to the Incas for its exceptional nutritional value, was believed to increase the stamina of their warriors. Quinoa is considered a complete protein, which makes it a perfect food for vegans and those on a gluten-free diet! This superfood is also high in B vitamins. Quinoa is a great substitute for typical rice dishes and adds more versatility to the kitchen. **Favorite Brand: Alter Eco Organic Royal Pearl Quinoa**

TAHINI. Made from ground sesame seeds, tahini is chock-full of calcium. Traditionally used in Middle Eastern cooking, tahini can be added to dips and dressings for a delicious, smooth, nutty taste. **Favorite Brand: Once Again Organic Sesame Tahini**

TAMARI. Like soy sauce, tamari is made from fermented soy. However, it differs from soy sauce in that it does not contain wheat. Due to the higher concentration of soy, you will notice a thicker, less salty taste. **Favorite Brand: San J's Organic Tamari**

TAPIOCA FLOUR. Also known as tapioca starch, this ingredient is often used in gluten-free baking to help the baked goods and improve the texture. Tapioca is believed to help with crispness and chew. Because it's not truly a nutritional powerhouse, I try to minimize my use of this starch whenever possible. **Favorite Brand: Bob's Red Mill Tapioca Flour**

Now let's get started!

CHAPTER 3

beginnings.

One of the best things about eating is when you are able to enjoy a long, leisurely meal with family and friends. It's a time to gather around the table, laugh, and just sit and enjoy the moment. What better way to kick off the night than with some fun appetizers to pair with your party cocktails? Here are some of my favorite recipes, ranging from scrumptious veggie rolls dipped in a spicy nut dressing to warm eggplant with a tasty romesco sauce. Appetizers don't need to be the typical bad-for-you pigs in the blanket (although that was my absolute favorite as a child) but rather healthy and decadent and always fun.

recipes

steamed artichoke

with sriracha aioli

. . . .

vegan, gluten-free

2 large artichoke hearts
1 lemon, cut in half
3 tbsp vegan mayonnaise
1 tbsp olive oil
1 clove garlic, minced
½ tsp Sriracha
Himalayan sea salt, to taste

Bring a large pot of water to a boil with half a lemon. Meanwhile, with a sharp knife, slice ½" off the top of each artichoke. Cut off the bottom of the stem, and peel the tough outer layer of the stem with a vegetable peeler. Cut off any remaining tough outer leaves. Cut the artichokes in half. Place artichokes in boiling water and simmer, covered for 30 minutes. In a small bowl, whisk together juice of one half of the lemon, mayo, oil, garlic, Sriracha, and salt. Serve.

brussels sprouts + apples on skewers

. . . .

vegan, gluten-free

1 lb Brussels sprouts
2 apples
olive oil
balsamic glaze
wooden kabob skewers

Preheat oven to 400°F. Cut Brussels sprouts in half, discarding outer skin. Cut apples into 1" pieces. Toss Brussels sprouts and apples in a bowl with a drizzle of oil. Put skewers though sprouts and apples. Place on a parchment-lined baking sheet and roast in the oven for 30 minutes. Serve with balsamic glaze drizzled on top.

vegetable rolls
with spicy nut sauce

vegan, gluten-free

Vegetable rolls are so beautiful and surprisingly easy once you get the hang of the first roll. Use any combination of veggies (or fruit!) to enjoy as an appetizer or even as a refreshing lunch.

8 rice paper sheets
2 avocados, sliced
½ cup shredded cucumber
½ cup shredded carrots
1 cup lettuce leaves

Spicy Nut Sauce:
⅓ cup nut butter, such as Nuttzo
2 cloves garlic, minced
1 tbsp ginger, minced
2 tbsp tamari
2 tbsp coconut sugar
3 tbsp water

Dip individual rice paper sheets into warm water to soften. Place veggies inside paper and fold the bottom to hold in fillings. Then fold in sides and roll tightly. Meanwhile, in a small bowl, whisk together sauce ingredients until smooth. Serve with sauce on the side.

roasted grapes, pistachio, goat cheese
+ truffle honey

. . . .

vegetarian, gluten-free

This is quite possibly one of my favorite appetizers to serve to guests. Not only is it beautiful, but it's also scrumptious and totally fun to eat. The grapes, pistachios, pecans, goat cheese, and truffle honey pair so wonderfully you would think they were made for one another. This is also great served as a dessert paired with a glass of dessert wine.

2 cups red seedless grapes, cut in half
½ cup pistachios
½ cup pecans
chèvre goat cheese
truffle honey

In a small skillet over medium heat, add grapes. Toss for 3–5 minutes until skin is slightly charred. Meanwhile, assemble plates with pistachios, pecans, and crumbled goat cheese. Add warm grapes on top and drizzle with truffle honey.

PURELY SCOOP
[CHEESE]

Cheese is one of those foods that can cause inflammation in the body, so I try to minimize it in my diet. However, it's believed that alternative sources to cow milk, such as goat or sheep, are easier for many of us to digest and provide some health benefits. Goat milk cheese is definitely one of my favorites and a staple in my fridge. There are so many varieties of goat milk cheese from chèvre, to feta, to a hard nutty cheese. Here are some of my favorites. Serve them with some fig jam and gluten-free crackers for the perfect appetizer.

VERMONT BUTTER AND CREAMERY—COUPLE

HAYSTACK FARM—FETA

CYPRESS GROVE—MIDNIGHT MOON

shishito peppers

. . . .

vegan, gluten-free

The first time I tasted a shishito pepper, I was walking through the Union Square Farm-ers Market in NYC where they were doing a cooking demonstration. I could not believe that a pepper, olive oil, and salt could have such robust flavor. But it was true. And to make matters even better, it is one of the easiest things to make. Move over edamame; there's a new green appetizer in town.

shishito peppers
olive oil
Himalayan sea salt
lemon

In a large bowl, toss peppers with olive oil. Heat a skillet to medium heat. Cook for 3–5 minutes per side then serve with a sprinkle of salt and squeeze of lemon.

roasted red pepper dip

....

vegan, gluten-free

The first time I tasted a friend's roasted red pepper dip, I thought I had died and gone to food heaven . . . or was it the good chardonnay paired with it?! Whatever it was, I think I ate enough to call it dinner. Mix and match peppers from the farmers' market, make a big batch, and if you happen to have any left over, freeze it!

3 red peppers
1 poblano pepper
1 spicy pepper, such as jalapeño
2 cloves garlic
¼ cup olive oil

Preheat oven to 400°F. Line a baking sheet with parchment paper. Place whole peppers and garlic in skin on baking sheet and roast for 35–40 minutes until peppers are charred. When peppers are cool enough to handle, discard stem and seeds. Place peppers, garlic, and olive oil in blender or food processor and blend until smooth. Serve with chips.

tip: instead of roasting in the oven, try grilling the peppers for an even better taste!

grilled polenta bites
with pistachio pesto + grilled tomatoes

vegan, gluten-free

I first made this recipe for a cooking class I taught in my sister's NYC apartment. Every month I taught a class of 10 or 12 twenty-something-year-old women. We spent the night cooking, eating, drinking, learning, and chatting. It was great. But the challenge was always how to make something super easy in a tiny kitchen with limited resources. I came up with this solution for a healthy holiday cooking class. The only difference was that I, of course, did not have a grill, so we put the assembled polenta under the broiler. You can do the same, but the grill definitely turns out better. Happy entertaining!

3 cups basil
1 clove garlic
½ cup pistachios
¼ cup fresh lemon juice
½ cup olive oil
Himalayan sea salt, to taste
18 oz, pre-cooked polenta log
grilled tomatoes
Parmesan (optional)

In a food processor, combine the basil, garlic, pistachios, lemon juice, and olive oil. Process until smooth. Add salt to taste. Set aside.

Preheat grill to medium-high heat. Slice the polenta into ¼" thick rounds and place on grill. Grill on each side for 3–5 minutes or until browned. When cooked, remove from grill. Assemble each round with a dollop of pesto, a grilled tomato, and a sprinkle of Parmesan (optional).

guacamole
with chipotle adobo sauce + goat cheese

....

vegetarian, gluten-free

This is my version of the guacamole served at Centro Latina in Boulder, Colorado. Fresh, spicy, and creamy, this guacamole makes for the perfect party app. I usually double or triple the recipe since guests seem to always gobble it up. Serve with traditional tortilla chips (of course, look for a variety with better-for-you ingredients) or with jicama slices (a root vegetable high in vitamin C and fiber) for an even cleaner option.

3 ripe avocados, cut in half with pit removed
1 clove of garlic, minced
¼ cup red onion, chopped
2 tbsp cilantro, minced
1–2 limes, juiced
1 tbsp olive oil
Himalayan sea salt to taste
1 can of chipotle peppers in adobo sauce
goat cheese to sprinkle on top

In a bowl, add avocado and mash with a fork, leaving chunky pieces. Add garlic, onion, cilantro, lime, olive oil, and salt. Stir to combine. Serve with chipotle peppers in adobo sauce and goat cheese sprinkled on top.

beet chips

. . . .

vegan, gluten-free

Instead of the typical bad-for-you fried chip, why not try baked beet chips? If you don't have a mandolin, be sure to use a great cutting knife so that you can thinly slice the beets for optimal crispness.

3 beets (mix of red and golden)
Himalayan sea salt or truffle salt
olive oil

Preheat oven to 350°F. Wash beets and remove skin with a peeler. Using a mandolin or sharp knife, cut beets into thin slices. Toss beets with olive oil and salt, placing red beet in one bowl and golden beets in another so the red color doesn't stain the golden beets. Place thin slices of beets on a parchment-lined baking sheet and bake in the oven for 35–45 minutes. Flip beets halfway through cooking. Serve.

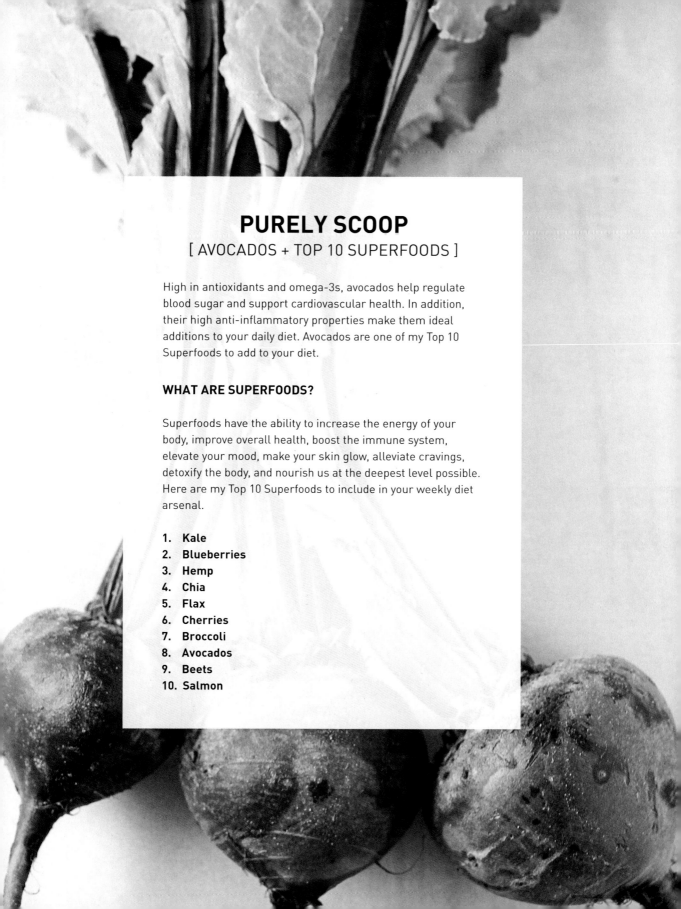

PURELY SCOOP
[AVOCADOS + TOP 10 SUPERFOODS]

High in antioxidants and omega-3s, avocados help regulate blood sugar and support cardiovascular health. In addition, their high anti-inflammatory properties make them ideal additions to your daily diet. Avocados are one of my Top 10 Superfoods to add to your diet.

WHAT ARE SUPERFOODS?

Superfoods have the ability to increase the energy of your body, improve overall health, boost the immune system, elevate your mood, make your skin glow, alleviate cravings, detoxify the body, and nourish us at the deepest level possible. Here are my Top 10 Superfoods to include in your weekly diet arsenal.

1. **Kale**
2. **Blueberries**
3. **Hemp**
4. **Chia**
5. **Flax**
6. **Cherries**
7. **Broccoli**
8. **Avocados**
9. **Beets**
10. **Salmon**

crostini two ways

I love these two fresh, seasonal crostini recipes. They are the perfect finger foods to serve for a cocktail party or casual dinner with friends.

fava bean crostini
with olive oil, parmesan + mint

. . . .

vegetarian, gluten-free

1 cup fava beans, cooked, skins discarded, roughly chopped
2 tbsp olive oil
2 cloves garlic, minced
2 tbsp chopped fresh mint
1 tbsp fresh lemon juice
Himalayan sea salt
8 slices gluten-free bread
½ cup Parmesan flakes, shaved

In a medium bowl, combine fava beans, olive oil, garlic, mint, lemon juice, and salt to taste. Spoon mixture on toasted or grilled slices of bread. Top with Parmesan flakes and serve.

grilled crostini
with strawberries, goat cheese + balsamic glaze

vegetarian, gluten-free

gluten-free baguette, sliced into ½" pieces
goat cheese
strawberries
balsamic glaze

Preheat grill to medium heat. Grill sliced baguette pieces 3 minutes per side. Assemble with a smear of goat cheese, sliced strawberries, and drizzle with balsamic glaze.

tip: swap the balsamic for chocolate sauce + you have a mouth-watering dessert!

cashew cheese mushroom ravioli

vegan, gluten-free

Cashews make the base for an incredible ricotta-like, cheese consistency. Seriously, no one will ever know these decadent raviolis aren't the "real" thing.

Ravioli:
1 cup arrowroot starch
¾ cup tapioca flour
½ cup brown rice flour
½ cup almond flour
1 tbsp xanthan gum
4 eggs
1 tbsp olive oil
1 tbsp water
1 jar tomato sauce

Mushroom Cashew Filling:
2 tbsp olive oil
¼ cup yellow onion, chopped
2 cloves garlic, minced
8 oz Portobello mushrooms
1 cup cashews, soaked in water
  for at least 4 hours
1 tbsp nutritional yeast
1 lemon, juiced
Himalayan sea salt, to taste

In the bowl of a mixer, mix dry ingredients together using the flat beater. Add eggs, water, and olive oil and mix on low speed for 3–4 minutes. Divide the dough into 6 balls. Place the rest of the dough in plastic wrap when not using so dough doesn't grow hard. Using a rolling pin coated in flour, roll each ball into rectangles thin enough to go through a pasta roller. Put the dough through the pasta roller and then cut with ravioli cutter.

In a large sauté pan, add 1 tbsp olive oil over medium heat. Add onion and garlic and sauté for 3–5 minutes. Add mushrooms and cook, stirring frequently for 10 minutes.

Meanwhile, in a high-speed blender, add drained cashews, 1 tbsp olive oil, nutritional yeast, and lemon juice. Blend until smooth. Add 1 tbsp at a time of water if necessary to reach desired consistency. Add the mushroom mixture and pulse a few times to combine. Add salt to taste. Fill the ravioli, placing a dollop of filling on the pasta, brush water or egg on the edges of the dough, place a layer of pasta on top and press edges together.

In a large pot, bring water to a boil. Cook the pasta for 3–5 minutes. Drain and set aside. Pour tomato sauce in pot and heat. Add in ravioli, coat with sauce, and serve.

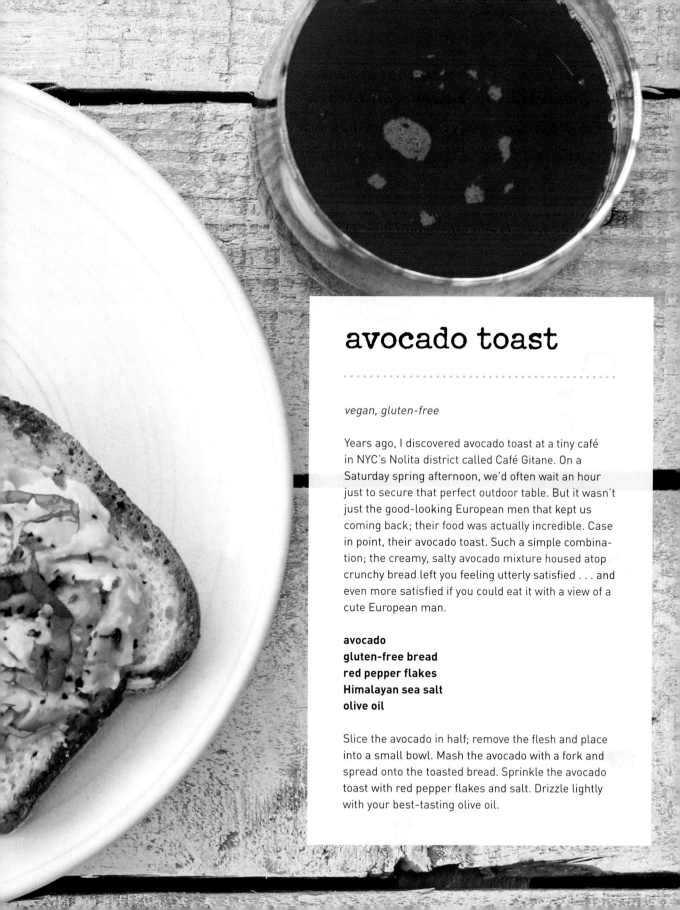

avocado toast

. . . .

vegan, gluten-free

Years ago, I discovered avocado toast at a tiny café
in NYC's Nolita district called Café Gitane. On a
Saturday spring afternoon, we'd often wait an hour
just to secure that perfect outdoor table. But it wasn't
just the good-looking European men that kept us
coming back; their food was actually incredible. Case
in point, their avocado toast. Such a simple combination; the creamy, salty avocado mixture housed atop
crunchy bread left you feeling utterly satisfied . . . and
even more satisfied if you could eat it with a view of a
cute European man.

avocado
gluten-free bread
red pepper flakes
Himalayan sea salt
olive oil

Slice the avocado in half; remove the flesh and place
into a small bowl. Mash the avocado with a fork and
spread onto the toasted bread. Sprinkle the avocado
toast with red pepper flakes and salt. Drizzle lightly
with your best-tasting olive oil.

sesame oil

PURELY SCOOP
[OIL]

There are so many oils on the market, how do you know which to choose from? All oils and fats are not created equal. Those high in omega-6s like sunflower and canola are definitely not your best friend. Instead, opt for the varieties that will help to nourish your body and skin. Don't be scared of fats. Good fats play a critical role in growth, reproduction, maintenance of skin tissue, and general body functioning. If you find that your skin is really dry, or you're really hungry throughout the day, without ever really feeling satisfied, you may need to add more fats to your diet. Here are a few of my favorites to look for. Be sure to always buy the highest quality you can find and store oils away from sunlight to prevent rancidity.

• **EXTRA VIRGIN OLIVE OIL**—best used for moderate stove top cooking and to drizzle on food before serving

• **UNREFINED COCONUT OIL**—best used for high temperature sautéing and baking

• **UNREFINED SESAME OIL**—best used unheated as a finishing oil

olive oil

coconut oil

grilled eggplant
with feta, romesco + mint

....

vegetarian, gluten-free

When I moved to Boulder, Colorado, one of the first restaurants I visited was Oak at Fourteenth. They have an incredible menu but one of the dishes in particular stood out— their grilled eggplant. The following recipe is my take on their dish. It is pretty much out of this world.

Romesco Sauce:
2 medium red bell peppers, halved and seeds removed
1 yellow onion, sliced
6 cloves garlic, peeled
4 tbsp tomato paste
2 tbsp olive oil
½ cup raw almonds
1 tsp sherry vinegar
1 tsp honey
1½ tsp smoked paprika
1 tsp Himalayan salt

2 eggplants, sliced lengthwise ¼" thick
olive oil
2 oz feta
½ cup basil, chiffonade

Preheat oven to 425°F. Place the peppers, onion, and garlic on a parchment-lined baking sheet. Drizzle with olive oil and roast in the oven. Remove garlic after about 30 minutes. Continue roasting peppers and onions for another 15 minutes.

When vegetables are done cooking, place them and the rest of the romesco ingredients in a food processor. Pulse until well combined, leaving some texture to the sauce. Pour into a bowl and set aside.

Meanwhile, coat eggplant in olive oil. Heat a grill to medium-high heat. Place sliced eggplant on grill and cook for 5 minutes each side. When eggplant is done, assemble each slice with a smear of romesco sauce, crumbled feta, and basil.

grilled zucchini boats
with chickpeas, tomatoes + artichokes

vegetarian, gluten-free

2 large zucchini, cut in half lengthwise
2 tbsp olive oil
1 clove garlic, minced
½ cup grape tomatoes, halved
½ cup marinated artichoke hearts, chopped
½ cup canned chickpeas
½ cup Parmesan cheese, shaved
basil

Scoop out the center of the zucchini, leaving about ½" of zucchini on the skin. Drizzle 1 tbsp olive oil over zucchini. Heat a grill to medium high heat. Place zucchini on grill and cook for 4–5 minutes per side. Meanwhile, in a skillet over medium heat, add 1 tbsp olive oil. Add garlic and sauté until fragrant, 2–3 minutes. Add tomatoes, artichokes, and chickpeas and sauté for 3–5 minutes. Fill the zucchini with vegetables and top with cheese and basil. Place back on the grill (or under the broiler) for another 5 minutes or until cheese is melted.

fire-roasted olives

vegan, gluten-free

1 cup pitted olives, Kalamata
½ cup pine nuts
½ cup golden raisins
¼ cup rosemary
1 tbsp olive oil

Heat a grill to medium heat. In aluminum foil, add olives, pine nuts, raisins, rosemary, and olive oil to the center of the foil. Fold up to create a packet. Grill over medium to high heat for 10–15 minutes.

hummus three ways

roasted pumpkin seed hummus

....

vegan, gluten-free

1½ cups pumpkin seeds
3 cloves garlic
½ cup olive oil, plus more for drizzling
1 tsp smoked paprika
1 (15-oz) can white beans, drained
1 lemon, juiced
1 tsp salt

Preheat oven to 350°F. On a parchment-lined baking sheet, add pumpkin seeds and spread evenly. Roast for 10–15 minutes. In a food processor, add roasted pumpkin seeds, garlic, olive oil, paprika, white beans, lemon juice, and salt. Blend until smooth. Adjust salt/olive oil to desired taste. Serve drizzled with olive oil and a sprinkle of smoked paprika.

pea hummus

antipasto plate with grilled artichokes, grilled asparagus, olives + cheese

. . . .

vegan, gluten-free

Nothing says spring has arrived as much as fresh peas at the farmers' market. Rather than traditional hummus using garbanzo beans, sub peas, or fava beans, for a fresh and light spring dip, make this hummus the center of the antipasto plate and serve with spring's other vegetables—grilled artichokes, asparagus, and some classic Kalamata olives and cheese.

3 tbsp tahini
2 cloves garlic
2 tbsp fresh lemon juice
2 cups peas
2 tbsp olive oil
Himalayan sea salt
¼ cup mint, chopped

Put tahini, garlic, lemon juice, peas, 1 tbsp olive oil, and sea salt to taste in a food processor and pulse until smooth. Drizzle with 1 tbsp of olive oil and chopped mint and serve.

roasted beet hummus

vegan, gluten-free

2 beets
¼ cup olive oil
2 tbsp tahini
1 (15-oz) can chickpeas, drained
½ tsp smoked paprika
1 clove garlic
gluten-free bread

Topping:
arugula
feta
pecans

Preheat oven to 425°F. Place each beet in aluminum foil. Roast for 40–50 minutes. When beets are done, remove foil covering and let them cool. When beets are cool enough to handle, rub off the skins and discard. Place roasted beets, oil, tahini, chickpeas, paprika, and garlic in a food processor and blend until smooth. Serve on gluten-free bread, topped with arugula, feta, and pecans.

roasted eggplant dip

vegan, gluten-free

2 eggplant, cut into ¼"–½" slices
4 tbsp olive oil
2 cloves garlic
3 tbsp tahini
½ tsp cumin
1 tsp salt
1 lemon, juiced
pomegranate seeds to garnish

Preheat oven to 375°F. On a parchment-lined baking sheet, place sliced eggplant and drizzle with 1 tbsp olive oil. Roast for 25 minutes. When eggplant has cooled, place all ingredients in a food processor. Pulse into creamy consistency. Serve with pomegranate seeds and a drizzle of olive oil.

white bean olive dip

vegan, gluten-free

Making your own dip is so simple and easy; just throw all the ingredients in a food processor and voila, you have a homemade dip.

¼ cup olive oil
1 (15-oz) can white beans, drained
1 clove garlic
1 lemon, juiced
½ tsp salt
¼ cup pitted Kalamata olives

Put olive oil, white beans, garlic, juice of lemon, salt, and olives in a food processor and pulse into smooth. Serve with chips.

[PURELY SCOOP: TORTILLA CHIPS]

You can make your own tortilla chips simply by cutting fresh tortillas, drizzling with olive oil, and baking in the oven for 10–15 minutes at 400°F. No frying, no weird ingredients, just pure.

crispy rice
with spicy tuna + avocado

gluten-free

This is one of my favorite apps to serve for guests. It's incredibly delicious and looks stunning. You can make a big batch of the crispy rice cakes and freeze for future use. Just pop them in the oven to reheat and top with tuna or avocado to serve.

2 cups sushi rice
2 tbsp rice vinegar
2 tbsp coconut sugar
2 tbsp toasted sesame oil
  (for cooking rice cakes)

Spicy Tuna Topping:
½ lb sushi-grade ahi tuna,
  cut into small cubes
½ tsp toasted sesame oil
1 tbsp Vegenaise
1 tbsp Sriracha
sliced jalapeño

Avocado Topping:
1 avocado, mashed
1 tsp toasted sesame oil
2 tsp tamari
sesame seeds

Cook the rice according to package directions. Combine rice vinegar and coconut sugar in a large bowl. Set aside.

Meanwhile make toppings:

Spicy Tuna: In a bowl, combine diced tuna, sesame oil, Vegenaise, and Sriracha.

Avocado Sesame: In a bowl, combine mashed avocado, sesame oil, and tamari.

When rice has cooled, form into tight compact patties. In a large sauté pan, heat oil over medium to high heat. Add rice patties in batches, cooking until golden brown, 2–3 minutes per side. Top with spicy tuna and jalapeño or avocado and sesame seed topping. Serve with tamari.

CHAPTER 4

salads.

Salads often get a bad reputation for being bland and boring. Not anymore! This chapter is my fresh take on salads—all loaded with nutrient-rich, superfood ingredients—and all ridiculously delicious. From the sweet, rich, grilled peach salad with burrata to a new twist on an emerging favorite—kale salad with strawberry, mint, jalapeño, lemon, lime, and shaved Parmesan—I hope you will be newly inspired to revisit this menu mainstay. In this chapter, I give you the tools to add more nutrient-rich leafy greens to your diet—one delicious salad at a time.

recipes

spring caprese salad with burrata, fava
beans + mint | 81

arugula salad with roasted beets,
pecans, corn, goat cheese + honey | 81

kale four ways:

1 | kale caesar salad with grilled
portobello + polenta croutons | 85

2 | kale + mache salad with grilled
artichoke + lemon dressing | 86

3 | spicy kale with strawberry, mint,
jalapeño + shaved parmesan | 89

4 | grilled kale salad with peaches, beets
+ burrata | 91

arugula with apples, pickled onions,
candied walnuts + manchego | 92

grilled watermelon + feta salad | 95

raw zucchini ribbon salad with arugula,
walnuts, lemon + basil | 95

beet green salad with feta, pine nuts
+ roasted beets | 96

grilled corn, avocado
+ tomato salad | 99

romaine heart salad with mint,
pecorino, cashews + roasted garlic
dressing | 100

mixed green salad with blackberries,
feta, walnuts + rice | 103

greek salad with buckwheat
+ grilled halloumi | 105

buckwheat autumn salad with
sweet potato + cranberries | 106

spring caprese salad with burrata, fava beans + mint

....

vegetarian, gluten-free

3 cups arugula
1 cup fava beans, cooked, skins discarded
1 tbsp mint, chiffonade
1 tbsp olive oil
1 lemon, juiced
zest from one lemon
4-oz ball of burrata
Himalayan sea salt, to taste
chili flakes

In a bowl, combine arugula, fava beans, mint, oil, lemon, and lemon zest. Toss to combine. Place on a plate with burrata. Season with salt and top with chili flakes.

arugula salad with roasted beets, pecans, corn, goat cheese + honey

....

vegetarian, gluten-free

The first time I had this salad was at a friend's BBQ in Boulder. I never had raw corn before and thought the combination was out of this world. I hope you feel the same!

5 baby beets
1 tbsp honey
1 tbsp olive oil
1 lemon, juiced
4 cups arugula
2 ears of corn, kernels scraped
⅓ cup pecans
¼ cup goat cheese

Preheat oven to 425°F. Discard beet leaves and wrap each beet in aluminum foil. Place on a baking sheet and roast for 45–50 minutes. When beets are finished cooking, open up foil and allow to cool. Meanwhile, in a small bowl, whisk together honey, oil, and lemon. Set aside. In a large bowl, assemble salad with arugula, corn, pecans, and crumbled goat cheese. Once beets are cool, use your hands to rub off skin. Cut beets in half and then into wedges and add to salad. Drizzle with dressing and serve.

PURELY SCOOP
[KALE + LEAFY GREENS]

Kale is the king of the leafy green family. Loaded with calcium
(1 cup of kale has the same amount of calcium as 1 cup of milk),
magnesium, iron, potassium, zinc, and vitamins A, C, E, and K.
In my mind, leafy greens deserve status as a superfood. Loaded
with fiber, chlorophyll, and other nutrients, they help detox the
body, strengthen the immune system, clear congestion, improve
circulation and bodily functions, and ultimately give you an overall
sense of greater well-being.

But kale isn't the only leafy green on the block. Some of my other
favorite greens include:

BOK CHOY—Typically used in Asian cuisine, bok choy is a member
of the cruciferous family, known to protect against cancer. With a
high water content, bok choy is best quickly stir-fried. Bok choy is
also loaded with vitamins C and A.

ARUGULA—As a member of the mustard family, arugula is
characterized by its pungent, spicy flavor. Mostly known as a salad
green, arugula is one of the most nutritious options for a salad
with higher levels of vitamin C, calcium, and beta-carotene than its
salad counterparts.

SPINACH—One of the most versatile greens, containing high
levels of vitamins A, C, and E. Spinach is quick-cooking (2–3
minutes) and is also wonderful raw in salads. It does contain oxalic
acid, which when released in cooking makes it difficult to absorb
calcium and iron.

SWISS CHARD—With an earthy, mild taste, Swiss chard can easily
be incorporated into a variety of recipes. The beautiful rainbow
stalks are high in vitamins A and C.

BEET GREENS—While beet greens are oftentimes discarded for
their bottom counterparts, they are actually more nutritious. High
in vitamin C, calcium, and iron, beet greens are super easy to cook
and can be substituted in any recipe that calls for cooked Swiss
chard or spinach.

kale four ways

kale caesar salad
with grilled portobello + polenta croutons

vegan, gluten-free

This is a fun vegan version of traditional Caesar salad. The grilled polenta croutons are absolutely delicious and certainly way healthier than any bread variety. Friends are always amazed by this healthier rendition and always ask for the recipe.

Caesar Dressing:
½ cup cashews,
    soaked for 2 hours
½ cup water
1 clove garlic, minced
1 tbsp olive oil
1 tbsp nutritional yeast
1 tsp Dijon mustard
1 tsp sherry vinegar
1 lemon
pinch of fine sea salt

2 large bunches of lacinato kale,
    tough stems removed and
    cut into thin shreds
1 tbsp olive oil
1 tbsp balsamic
2 large portobello caps
1 polenta log, sliced
    lengthwise ½" thick

Place all dressing ingredients in a high-speed blender or food processor. Blend until smooth, adding more water if necessary. Place kale in a large salad bowl and toss with Caesar dressing. Meanwhile, heat a grill to medium heat. In a bowl, add olive oil and balsamic. Toss the portobello mushrooms in marinade then place on the grill along with the polenta slices. Grill on each side for 3–5 minutes. Remove food from grill and allow to cool. Slice mushrooms and cut polenta into cubes. Toss salad with mushrooms and polenta and serve.

kale + mache salad
with grilled artichoke + lemon dressing

vegetarian, gluten-free

Mache is a European salad green known for its sweet taste. Paired with kale, lemon, and grilled artichokes, this salad is so refreshing and flavorful, it will leave you craving the combo again. I've definitely been known to eat this salad daily for weeks.

2 large bunches of lacinato kale, tough stems removed and cut into thin shreds
2 cups mache
1–2 cloves garlic, minced
2 tbsp lemon juice
2 tbsp olive oil
½ cup Parmesan cheese
salt to taste
1 cup marinated artichoke hearts

In a bowl, combine kale, mache, garlic, lemon juice, olive oil, and Parmesan cheese and salt. Toss thoroughly to combine. Meanwhile, heat a skillet or grill over medium heat. Add marinated artichoke hearts. Cook on each side until brown, 2–3 minutes each. Serve salad with warm artichokes on top.

spicy kale

with strawberry, mint, jalapeño + shaved parmesan

. . . .

vegetarian, gluten-free

**2 large bunches of lacinato kale,
  tough stems removed and cut
  into thin shreds**
1 tbsp olive oil
½ lemon, juiced
1 lime, juiced
Himalayan sea salt
1 cup sliced strawberries
½ cup shaved Parmesan cheese
3 tbsp fresh mint, chopped
**1 small jalapeño, deseeded
  and thinly sliced**

In a large bowl, add shredded kale, oil, lemon juice, lime juice, and salt. Toss thoroughly to combine. Add strawberries, Parmesan, mint, and jalapeños. Toss to combine.

tip: swap out peaches for other delicious grilled fruits like plums, grapefruit, or watermelon.

grilled kale salad
with peaches, beets + burrata

....

vegetarian, gluten-free

There's nothing better than peaches cooked on the grill. I absolutely love this salad with its variety of tastes and textures. The peaches and beets pair beautifully with the creamy burrata. Yes, burrata would be part of the 20, in the 80/20 Rule.

2 beets, peeled
   and cut into thin slices
1 tbsp olive oil
Himalayan sea salt
1 bunch of lacinato kale
2 peaches, cut in half
1 (8-oz) ball of burrata
¼ cup pistachios

Dressing:
2 tbsp olive oil
2 tbsp balsamic vinegar
1 tsp maple syrup
Himalayan sea salt

Preheat grill to medium-high heat. Toss the beets with ½ tbsp olive oil and sprinkle with salt. In a separate bowl, toss kale with ½ tbsp olive oil and sprinkle with salt. Spread kale on the grill and cook on each side for 2–3 minutes or until the edges are crispy. Grill beets and peaches for 5 minutes per side. Set all vegetables and fruit aside. Transfer the kale to a cutting board and remove the center stems. Assemble the plate with kale, peaches, beets, sliced burrata, and a sprinkle of pistachios. In a small bowl, whisk together dressing ingredients. Serve salad with dressing drizzled on top.

arugula

with apples, pickled onions, candied walnuts + manchego

. . . .

vegetarian, gluten-free

Arugula carries a peppery taste. When mixed with sweet candied walnuts, pickled onions, and nutty sheep milk manchego, it's a match made in salad heaven. Though there are several steps to making the salad, it's definitely worth it. You can make a big batch of both the onions and walnuts and save for another day.

4 cups arugula
1/3 cup pickled onions
1/3 cup apple, julienned
1/3 cup manchego cheese, diced
1/3 cup candied walnuts
2 tbsp sherry vinegar
1 tbsp walnut oil
1 tbsp olive oil
1 tbsp chopped shallot
1/2 tsp Himalayan sea salt

In a large bowl, combine arugula, onions, apple, cheese, and walnuts. In a small bowl, whisk together vinegar, oils, shallots, and salt. Pour dressing over salad and toss to combine.

Pickled Onions:
1 red onion, sliced
1/2 tsp coconut sugar
1/2 tsp salt
1/4 cup rice vinegar
1/4 cup apple cider vinegar
1/4 cup sherry vinegar
2 small cloves garlic, peeled

In a small pot, bring 2 cups of water to a boil. Place onions in a colander. When water comes to a boil, slowly pour water over the onions to soften. In a glass container, add sugar, salt, vinegars, garlic, and onions. Cover and shake to combine. The onions will be ready in about 30 minutes but are better with time. Store in the refrigerator.

Candied Walnuts:
1/3 cup coconut sugar
1/4 cup water
2 tbsp coconut oil
1 1/2 cups walnut halves

Combine first 3 ingredients in a large skillet. Bring to boil, whisking for 1 minute. Add walnuts and stir for about 3 minutes. Transfer nuts to parchment-lined baking sheet and allow to cool.

PURELY SCOOP
[APPLE CIDER VINEGAR]

Apple cider vinegar has been used for centuries for its many healing properties. It's a versatile staple to stock in your pantry. My favorite brand is Bragg, which is also raw and organic. Here are a few great uses for the vinegar.

• Use as a base in fermenting veggies

• Mix with milk to create a healthier "buttermilk"

• Rinse in your hair after shampooing to create shine

• Dab on your face to balance pH

• Drink with water to balance the body's pH

• Create a nontoxic cleaning agent for the home

• Keep rooms smelling clean with a bowl left in a stinky area

• Sip with water to relieve an upset stomach

grilled watermelon + feta salad

. . . .

vegetarian, gluten-free

Watermelon and feta find each other often in salad combinations. Here, I grill the watermelon for a twist on the traditional combo. During the summer months, watermelon is great to keep your body hydrated, plus it's a good source of lycopene, which helps fight inflammation.

1 watermelon
2 limes
1 cup feta
balsamic glaze
arugula
Himalayan sea salt

Cut watermelon into 1" slices. Squeeze lime over the watermelon and set aside. Heat a grill to medium heat. Place watermelon on grill, 5 minutes per side. Cut feta into 1" slices. Assemble on plate, alternating with watermelon and feta. Drizzle with balsamic glaze, arugula, and sprinkle with sea salt. Serve.

raw zucchini ribbon salad
with arugula, walnuts, lemon + basil

. . . .

vegetarian, gluten-free

Here, this simple, fresh salad takes on the flavor of zesty lemon and tangy goat cheese. It's the perfect side dish to a summer feast.

Dressing:
1 lemon, juiced
½ tbsp olive oil
½ tsp salt
½ tsp sherry vinegar

2 zucchini
1 cup arugula
¼ cup basil, chiffonade
⅓ cup walnuts
⅓ cup goat cheese crumbles

Place dressing ingredients in a small bowl and whisk to combine. Cut zucchini into ribbons using a vegetable peeler. In a large bowl, add zucchini, arugula, basil, walnuts, and goat cheese. Pour in dressing and toss to combine. Serve.

beet green salad
with feta, pine nuts + roasted beets

vegetarian, gluten-free

A nutritional powerhouse, beets not only help the body to detox but also provide high amounts of antioxidants and anti-inflammatory properties. Most of us think to discard beets' leafy greens, but you can actually eat them and prepare them like you would spinach or Swiss chard.

2 large red beets, with greens attached
2 tbsp olive oil
1 clove garlic, minced
½ small onion, chopped
1 tbsp balsamic vinegar
4 oz goat milk feta cheese
3 tbsp pine nuts

Preheat oven to 425°F. Wash beets, leaving the skins on. Remove the greens and set aside. Wrap beets individually in aluminum foil with a drizzle of oil. Bake for 45–60 minutes, depending on size. When the beets are done cooking, remove skin and cut into slices. Meanwhile, cut beet greens into shredded pieces, removing large stems. Heat 1 tbsp of olive oil in a skillet over medium heat. Add garlic and onion and sauté until fragrant for 5–7 minutes. Stir in greens and cook until slightly wilted, 3–5 minutes. Pour in vinegar and stir to coat. Assemble salad with beet greens as the base, sliced beets, feta cheese, and pine nuts.

grilled corn, avocado + tomato salad

. . . .

vegan, gluten-free

This simple summery salad is the perfect example of farm-fresh eating. With summer's sweet corn and tomatoes, this salad really doesn't need too much more.

2 ears of corn
2 cups grape tomatoes, halved
1 avocado, diced
1 tbsp olive oil
1 clove garlic, minced
1 lime, juiced

Remove husks from corn and grill over medium heat for 10 minutes. Cut the corn off the cob with a knife. Set aside and let cool. When cooled, combine with the remaining ingredients in a bowl and serve.

romaine heart salad
with mint, pecorino, cashews + roasted garlic dressing

. . . .

vegetarian, gluten-free

Roasted Garlic Dressing:
¼ cup water
⅓ cup olive oil
3 lemons
3 roasted garlic cloves
½ tsp mustard
⅓ cup walnuts
salt

4 romaine hearts
2 tbsp mint, chopped
¼ cup pecorino romano, grated
¼ cup cashews
2 tbsp hemp seeds

In a food processor or high-speed blender, blend dressing ingredients until smooth. On a large plate, assemble salad with romaine hearts, sprinkled with mint, pecorino, cashews, and hemp seeds. Drizzle dressing over salad and serve.

PURELY SCOOP
[SEEDS]

I love to have a variety of seeds stocked in my pantry to sprinkle on top of breakfast, lunch, and dinner. Seeds pack a powerful nutritional punch for their tiny size. Here are a few of my staples:

SUNFLOWER SEEDS are an excellent source of vitamin E. Vitamin E is a critical antioxidant that neutralizes free radicals in the body and promotes anti-inflammatory effects.

PUMPKIN SEEDS, or pepitas, are high in zinc, iron, potassium, and magnesium. Studies show that magnesium helps to calm and expand the muscles helping to reduce such things as asthma and migraine headaches and lower high blood pressure.

SESAME SEEDS are high in both copper and calcium. Trading in dairy? Try adding sesame seeds to your meals. With just 2 tablespoons of sesame seeds, you receive 200 milligrams of calcium. That is almost as much as a glass of milk, which contains 300 milligrams.

HEMP SEEDS were first used in China more than six thousand years ago as a staple food. Rich in omega-3 fatty acids and protein, hemp seeds are considered a perfect food. This superfood is also rich in sulfur, known as the beauty mineral, as well as iron and vitamin E. I love throwing hemp seeds on top of salad, soups, cereals, even pasta for added nutrition, crunch, and nutty flavor.

CHIA SEEDS are a powerful superfood once used as currency for their exceptional value. The Aztec warriors used this endurance seed, rich in omega-3 fatty acids, fiber, and protein to run great distances. Studies show that eating chia seeds slows down how fast our bodies convert carbohydrate calories into simple sugars. Look for Salba® Chia, the most nutritionally consistent and nutrient-dense form of chia on the planet.

FLAXSEEDS are high in omega-3s, fiber, and protein. Flaxseeds can be consumed both ground and whole. Sprinkle them on your salad, smoothie, or in baked goods.

mixed green salad
with blackberries, feta, walnuts + rice

....

vegetarian, gluten-free

Loaded with blackberries and fresh mint, this light, refreshing salad is perfect to serve on a warm summer's day. Want some extra protein? This salad is simply delicious served with the quinoa-crusted chicken on page 202.

4 cups mixed greens
¼ cup feta (Haystack is amazing)
¼ cup walnuts, chopped
1½ cups brown rice, cooked
½ cup blackberries
1 sprig of mint, chopped

Dressing:
¼ cup blackberries
2 tbsp olive oil
1 tbsp balsamic vinegar

In a large bowl, assemble the salad with mixed greens, feta, walnuts, rice, blackberries, and mint. In a high-speed blender, add dressing ingredients and blend until smooth. Drizzle salad with dressing and serve.

greek salad
with buckwheat + grilled halloumi

. . . .

vegetarian, gluten-free

Halloumi is a Greek cheese traditionally made from goat and sheep milk. Its tangy, salty flavor pairs perfectly with this Greek salad. Serve with a glass of rosé for a perfect light summer's dinner.

1 medium red onion, halved and thinly sliced
3 tomatoes, cut into wedges
1 cucumber, peeled and cut into chunks
1 green bell pepper, seeded and sliced
1 red bell pepper, seeded and sliced
½ cup pitted and halved Kalamata olives
1 cup buckwheat, cooked
6 oz halloumi, sliced

Dressing Ingredients:
¼ cup red wine vinegar
¼ cup extra virgin olive oil
2 large cloves garlic, minced
handful of fresh parsley, chopped
1 lemon, juiced
Himalayan sea salt, to taste
freshly ground black pepper

In a large bowl, combine onions, tomatoes, cucumbers, peppers, olives, and buckwheat. In a small bowl, whisk together dressing ingredients. Pour onto salad and toss to combine. Meanwhile, place the halloumi on a grill or skillet for 3 minutes per side or until browned. Serve salad with grilled halloumi on top.

buckwheat autumn
salad with sweet potato + cranberries

vegan, gluten-free

Dressing:
2 tbsp maple syrup
2 tbsp apple cider vinegar
1 tbsp balsamic vinegar
4 tbsp olive oil
1 tsp mustard
pinch of Himalayan sea salt

2 cups buckwheat, cooked
1 lb sweet potato, roasted and cubed
½ cup dried cranberries
4 cups arugula
½ cup walnuts

In a small bowl, whisk together dressing ingredients. Set aside. In a large bowl, combine buckwheat, sweet potatoes, cranberries, arugula, and walnuts. Toss with dressing and serve.

CHAPTER 5

soups.

There's no better way to add loads of fresh, vitamin-packed vegetables to your diet than in scrumptious, satisfying soups. This chapter brings together my favorite quick and delicious soups that can be enjoyed throughout the year. From the rich, complex broth of red lentil coconut curry soup to my flavorful, hearty take on veggie chili, all are great additions to a meal or, in some cases, make an excellent, satisfying meal themselves.

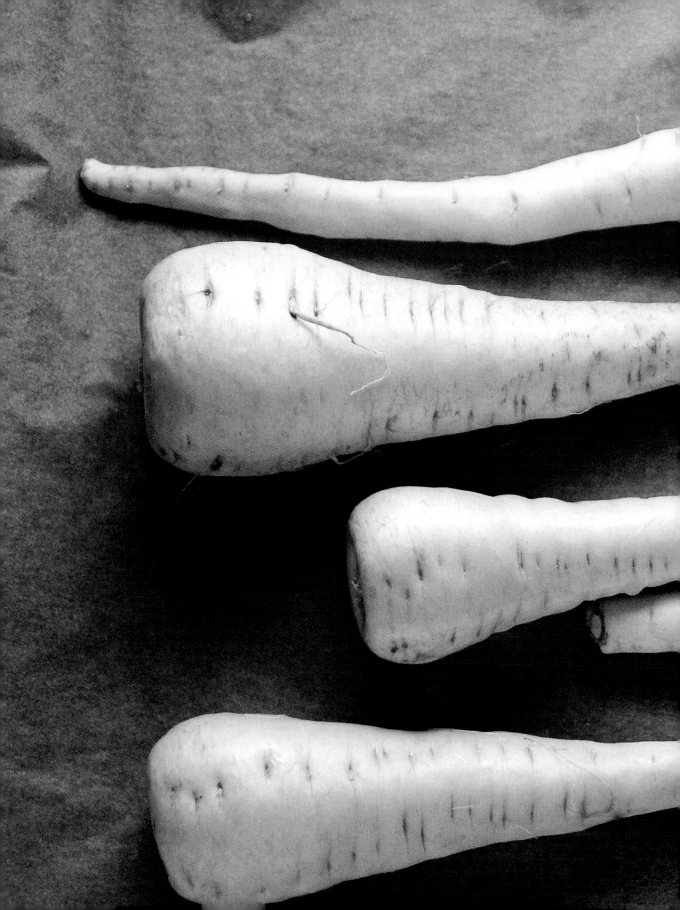

recipes

roasted parsnip, garlic + apple soup

....

vegetarian, gluten-free

2 tbsp olive oil
1 lb parsnips
1 head garlic
1 yellow onion, diced
1 gala apple, diced
1 (15-oz) can white beans, drained
32 oz vegetable stock
Himalayan sea salt

Toppings:
pumpkin seed oil
Parmesan cheese
rosemary

Preheat oven to 400°F. On a parchment-lined baking sheet, drizzle ½ tbsp olive oil over parsnips. Slice off the top of the head of garlic, so that each clove inside is exposed. Drizzle 1 tbsp of olive oil and wrap in foil. Roast the garlic and parsnips for 45 minutes. Chop cooked parsnips. Meanwhile, in a large pot, heat remaining olive oil. Add diced onions and sauté for 3–5 minutes until fragrant. Add apple, parsnips, garlic (skin removed), and white beans. Sauté for 5–7 minutes. Add vegetable stock and bring to a low simmer for 15 minutes. Using an immersion blender, blend until smooth. Season with salt and serve with drizzled pumpkin seed oil, Parmesan cheese, and fresh rosemary.

broccoli potato soup

....

vegan, gluten-free

This is one of the most flavorful broccoli soups I've ever had. It seems like it's made with heavy cream, but instead I've swapped the unhealthy fats for coconut milk and vegan butter. This can certainly be a meal unto itself, especially with some gluten-free toast on the side. This is the perfect meal for a cold winter's day. Broccoli, one of my top superfoods, helps to detoxify the body and is loaded with fiber, vitamins C, A, E, and K.

3 tbsp vegan butter
1 medium onion, chopped
1 tsp dry mustard
6 cups of broccoli, chopped
2 large red bliss potatoes, chopped
4 cups vegetable stock
¾ cup coconut milk
salt, to taste

In a large pot over medium heat, melt butter. Add onion and dry mustard, stirring until onion is soft, 3–5 minutes. Add broccoli and potatoes; continue to cook for 5–7 minutes, stirring often. Add vegetable stock and coconut milk, bring to a boil, then reduce heat and simmer for 30 minutes. Using an immersion blender or regular blender, blend until smooth.

creamy asparagus soup

. . . .

vegan, gluten-free

This is the perfect soup to serve at the first signs of spring. Somehow this always makes its way onto a Sunday brunch menu. I love serving this in shot glasses for an easy, light appetizer to start off a meal. Serve warm or cold and enjoy.

1 tbsp coconut oil
1 onion
2 cloves garlic, minced
1 large bundle of asparagus, ends trimmed
2 cups vegetable broth
1 cup coconut milk
salt

In a medium-sized pot, heat oil over low to medium heat. Add onion, garlic, and asparagus and sauté for 5–7 minutes. Add broth and coconut milk and simmer on low for 10–15 minutes. Using an immersion blender or high-speed blender, purée until smooth. Add salt to taste.

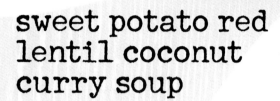

sweet potato red lentil coconut curry soup

vegan, gluten-free

On a chilly day, this lentil soup warms up the body immediately. Not to mention, it makes your house smell divine. This hearty soup is packed with iron and protein from the lentils, making this a great vegetarian powerhouse meal.

**3 sweet potatoes, peeled and diced into
small pieces**
2 tbsp olive oil
1 tbsp fresh grated ginger
1 onion, diced
1 clove garlic, minced
4 cups vegetable stock
1 (15-oz) can coconut milk
1½ tbsp red curry paste
1 (15-oz) can crushed tomatoes
1 cup red or yellow lentils
salt to taste

Preheat oven to 425°F. Toss sweet potatoes with 1 tbsp of olive oil and roast for 25 minutes. Meanwhile, in a medium pot, sauté the ginger, onion, and garlic in oil until softened. Add all the other ingredients and simmer, covered, for 25 minutes. Add roasted sweet potatoes and continue to simmer for 10–15 minutes. Use an immersion blender (or food processor) to blend until smooth or to desired consistency.

white bean kale soup
with pumpkin seed pesto

vegan, gluten-free

I made this soup for the first time before a personal best 10k race. It's now a staple. It has the perfect components to fuel your body before a race. Loaded with veggies, plant-based protein, and carbs, this soup will leave you feeling light, yet satisfied. Serve with a slice of gluten-free toast to soak up all the yumminess.

1 tbsp olive oil
2 cloves garlic, minced
½ cup chopped onion
1 (15-oz) can of white beans, drained
2 cups chopped kale
32 oz vegetable broth
Himalayan sea salt, to taste

Pumpkin Seed Pesto:
2 cups basil
½ cup olive oil
¼ cup pumpkin seeds
2 cloves garlic
½ lemon, juiced
Himalayan sea salt to taste

In a pot, heat olive oil over low to medium heat. Add garlic and sauté until fragrant. Add the onion and sauté until translucent (5–7 minutes). Add the white beans, kale, and broth and simmer on low to medium heat for 15 minutes. Meanwhile, in a food processor, add all the pesto ingredients and blend until smooth. When ready to serve, drizzle pumpkin seed pesto on top of soup.

PURELY SCOOP
[PLANT-BASED PROTEINS, BEANS + LEGUMES]

Protein is essential for the body to function optimally. Protein is responsible for the growth, repair, and maintenance of muscles in your body. It also plays a role in building healthy nails, skin, and hair. Protein boosts your metabolism and enhances your immune system by producing antibodies to fight disease. Including enough protein in your diet will keep you feeling full longer and can help curb cravings for sweets.

When following a plant-based diet, be sure to include protein-rich beans and legumes. Not only are beans and legumes high in protein, but also fiber, iron, magnesium, and potassium. Here are a few of my favorites . . .

LENTILS—They are the fastest-cooking of the legumes; colors include green, brown, red, and yellow. Lentils are great for salads, and soup.

BLACK BEANS—High in magnesium and fiber, black beans often mix well with spicy flavorings like garlic, lime, cumin, and cilantro. They are a perfect addition to any Mexican feast.

GARBANZO BEANS—Garbanzo beans, or chickpeas, are a good protein and iron source most often used in hummus, but I love adding them to pasta dishes, soups, and salads.

ADZUKI BEANS—In Chinese medicine, adzuki beans are thought to have healing effects in the body, particularly to the kidneys. Adzuki beans can be used in chili or in recipes where you would typically use kidney beans.

gazpacho two ways

tomato gazpacho

vegan, gluten-free

My mom has been making this recipe for years. During the summer, she always has a big batch in the fridge waiting for us to eat as soon as we took a lunch break from the beach. It's the perfect fuel to eat before heading back into the sun.

1 cucumber
2 red peppers
2 tomatoes
1 red onion
2 cloves garlic
1 (32-oz) tomato juice
¼ cup olive oil
¼ cup balsamic vinegar
½ tsp Himalayan sea salt
1 avocado, diced

Place all but the last ingredient in a food processor. Blend until desired consistency with some small pieces. Serve with diced avocado on top.

white gazpacho

vegan, gluten-free

This is a fun take on your typical tomato-based gazpacho soup. The cucumbers make this super cooling and the perfect refreshment to a hot summer's day.

1 large cucumber, peeled, seeded, and chopped
1¼ cups seedless green grapes
¼ cup blanched almonds
¼ cup almond milk, unsweetened
½ clove garlic
½ tbsp shallot, chopped
1 tbsp red wine vinegar
2 tbsp flaxseed
½ tsp Himalayan sea salt
½ cup tomatoes, chopped

Put cucumber, grapes, almonds, almond milk, garlic, shallot, red wine vinegar, and flaxseed into a blender and purée until smooth, about 2 minutes. The finished texture should be smooth, creamy, and just a bit grainy from the almonds. Season to taste with salt, then transfer gazpacho to a bowl. Cover and refrigerate until well chilled. When ready to serve, pour gazpacho into bowls and garnish with sliced tomatoes.

tomato, chickpea + amaranth soup

. . . .

vegan, gluten-free

1 tbsp olive oil
3 cloves garlic, minced
1 onion, chopped
¼ tsp cumin
¼ tsp smoked paprika
1 tbsp balsamic vinegar
1 cup cooked amaranth
1 cup vegetable stock
2 tbsp tomato paste
1 (15-oz) can chickpeas,
    drained and rinsed
1 (28-oz) can chopped tomatoes
Himalayan sea salt, to taste

Heat olive oil in a large pot over medium heat. Add garlic, onions, and spices and sauté until fragrant, 2–3 minutes. Add remaining ingredients and bring to a boil. Reduce heat and simmer for 25 minutes. Serve.

veggie chili

. . . .

vegan, gluten-free

Hearty, spicy, and delicious, this veggie chili reminds me of snowy days cuddled inside. My mom still makes this when I go home and always makes a big batch for me to put in my freezer. Serve with gluten-free skillet-baked corn bread (page 312) on the side for an added flavor bonus.

⅓ cup olive oil
2 cups mushrooms
1 cup red peppers, chopped
1 cup carrots, chopped
2 cups onions, chopped
3 cloves garlic, minced
1 tsp red pepper flakes
1 tsp cumin
2½ tbsp canned green chilies
2 tsp chili powder
1 quart tomato juice or more if needed
1 cup cooked brown rice
1 (15-oz) can diced tomatoes
1 (20-oz) can adzuki beans, drained
3 tbsp tomato paste

Heat olive oil in large pot over medium high heat; add mushrooms, red peppers, carrots, onion, garlic, and spices. Cook for 5–7 minutes. Add remaining ingredients. Bring to a boil and stir. Reduce the heat and simmer 25–30 minutes, uncovered. Add salt to taste.

tip: sautéing the spices first helps to bring out their full flavor in this soup.

creamy mushroom soup
with pine nuts + truffle

....

vegan, gluten-free

The key to making this soup taste absolutely delicious is sautéing the mushrooms for a long time at a low temperature. The flavors emerge, and you are left with a rich, delicious soup. I love adding shiitake mushrooms to the mix as they are a good source of iron and good for your immune system.

1 tbsp olive oil
3 cloves garlic, finely chopped
1 large shallot, finely chopped
2 lbs assorted mushrooms
3 cups of vegetable broth
1 (15-oz) can coconut milk
truffle sea salt, to taste
pine nuts

In a pot over medium heat, add olive oil, garlic, and shallot. Sauté for 3–5 minutes or until fragrant. Add mushrooms and continue to sauté for 20–30 minutes on low to medium heat. Add broth and cream of the coconut milk, discarding the coconut liquid. Using an immersion blender, blend until smooth. Continue to cook on low for 10 minutes. Add truffle salt to taste and top with pine nuts.

roasted
carrot soup

vegan, gluten-free

2 tbsp olive oil
1 medium onion, chopped
4 cloves garlic, minced
¼ tsp coriander
½ tsp cumin
2 lbs carrots
4 cups vegetable broth
1 (15-oz) can coconut milk
2 tsp salt

Heat olive oil in large pot over medium heat. Add onion, garlic, coriander, and cumin and sauté until fragrant, 3–5 minutes. Add carrots and sauté for 10–15 minutes. Add broth and coconut milk then cover pot with lid. Simmer for 30 minutes. Purée soup in a blender or with an immersion blender until smooth.

veggie mains.

Vegetarian dishes seem to get a bad reputation for being the healthier, but not necessarily the tastier, choice. Hopefully this chapter will prove that theory wrong. I love serving these hearty, flavor-rich vegetarian entrées to steak-and-potato dinner guests and hearing their surprise as they leave feeling full, happy, and totally satisfied.

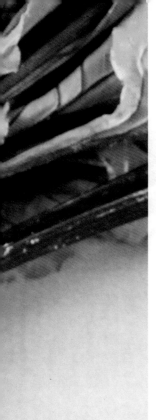

recipes

black bean beet burger

vegetarian, gluten-free

3 large red beets
1 tbsp olive oil
1 yellow onion, diced
3 cloves garlic, minced
¼ cup Purely Elizabeth Ancient Grain
    Original Oatmeal
1 (15-oz) can black beans, rinsed and drained
1 cup cooked millet
¼ cup barbecue sauce, such as Stubbs
1 large egg, optional for non-vegan burger

Toppings:
arugula
feta
beet hummus (page 71)

Preheat oven to 425°F. Place each beet in aluminum foil. Roast for 40–50 minutes. When beets are done, remove foil covering and let them cool. When beets are cool enough to handle, rub off the skins and discard.

In a large skillet, heat olive oil to medium heat. Add onion and garlic and sauté for 10 minutes. Set aside. Meanwhile, in a food processor, add beans and oatmeal and pulse. Set aside in a large bowl. Add peeled beets to food processor and process until smooth. Pour beets into black bean and oatmeal mixture. Add millet, onions, garlic, BBQ sauce, and egg. Mix well. Refrigerate the mixture. Form into patties and cook on an olive oil–lined large skillet over medium heat. Cook for 3–5 minutes per side. Serve on gluten-free bread with arugula, feta, and beet hummus.

risotto
with leeks + asparagus

vegetarian, gluten-free

Traditionally, risotto is one heck of a heavy, creamy dish. To help make this a bit more purely friendly, I've eliminated the pounds of cheese and subbed in our 6-grain hot cereal for white rice. The 6 grains and seeds increase fiber, protein and omega-3s, which help keep you feeling full longer and help fight inflammation.

1 tbsp olive oil
2 cloves garlic, minced
1 cup leeks, chopped
1 bunch of asparagus, trimmed,
    cut in 2" pieces
1 cup Purely Elizabeth Ancient 6-Grain
    Hot Cereal
½ cup white wine
32 oz veggie broth

Toppings:
basil
asiago cheese

In a large saucepan over medium heat, add olive oil and garlic. Sauté until fragrant, 2–3 minutes. Add leeks and asparagus and cook for 3–5 minutes. Add 6-grain hot cereal and sauté for 2 minutes. Add wine. In ½-cup increments, start adding the vegetable broth, stirring constantly. Once the grains have absorbed the broth, add the next ½ cup and continue to stir. Risotto should cook in about 40 minutes. When the risotto is finished cooking, top with chopped basil and asiago cheese and serve.

PURELY SCOOP
[VEGETABLES]

The one thing missing most from Americans' diets are vegetables. Vegetables are especially helpful if you find that you're feeling a bit more sluggish or are putting on weight instead of losing it. They are nutrient-dense (loaded with vitamins and fiber) and low in calories and fat. Because of this, you can munch on them all day long! Vegetables also help ease digestion and give you more regularity in your elimination cycle.

WHICH VEGETABLES ARE BEST?

1. THE SWEET VEGGIES (squash, yams, beets, carrots, and parsnips): These vegetables curb sweet cravings and help smooth digestion.

2. THE FAT DISSOLVERS (daikon, scallions, leeks, radishes): These vegetables will help break up mucous and fat in your body.

3. GREEN LEAFY VEGGIES (kale, watercress, collard greens, Swiss chard, spinach, etc.): These are nutritional powerhouses!

4. CRUCIFEROUS VEGGIES (broccoli, cauliflower, cabbage): These veggies are known to prevent cancer and contain lots of insoluble fiber.

purely

pad thai
with maple ginger sauce

. . . .

vegan, gluten-free

Most pad thai dishes that you find in restaurants are loaded with bad-for-you oils and other scary ingredients. So I've recreated a traditional pad thai that won't leave you feeling full and sluggish. This one is full of flavor and good-for-you ingredients. Sub the peanut butter with your favorite nut butter, like Nuttzo, a seven-seed and nut butter loaded with the good stuff!

6 oz brown rice fettuccine noodles
1 tbsp coconut oil
2 cloves garlic, minced
½ tbsp ginger, minced
1 cup onion, diced
2 cups mushrooms, chopped
1 cup carrots, chopped
1 medium head of broccoli, cut into florets
1 lime
scrambled egg, optional

Sauce Ingredients:
2 tbsp tamari
2 tbsp nut butter, such as Nuttzo
½ tbsp maple syrup

Cook rice noodles according to package instructions. Heat a large skillet to medium heat. Add oil, garlic, and ginger; sauté until fragrant 2–3 minutes. Add chopped onions and sauté for 2 minutes. Stir in mushrooms, carrots, and broccoli and continue to sauté until desired tenderness is reached. Meanwhile, in a small bowl, whisk together sauce ingredients. Add cooked rice noodles and sauce to the skillet; stir until evenly coated. Serve with a squeeze of lime.

PURELY SCOOP
[ANCIENT GRAINS]

QUINOA—A complete protein, this superfood has almost twice as much fiber as other grains. Quinoa promotes digestion, lowers cholesterol and glucose levels, and contains a slew of vitamins and minerals including iron (promotes brain health) and lysine (essential for tissue growth and repair).

AMARANTH—Amaranth was a favorite of the Aztecs for its high nutritional value and ability to thrive in poor soil. It's high in protein, the amino acid lysine, calcium, and B vitamins.

KANIWA—Also known as quinoa's baby cousin, kaniwa is high in protein, fiber, iron, and calcium. Unlike quinoa, it does not contain any saponins (which have a bitter flavor) and has a slightly nutty, sweet taste. About half the size of quinoa, Kaniwa grows in the same harsh environment in Peru and Bolivia.

MILLET—This is an ancient grain, rich in B vitamins, that helps support metabolism, increase immunity, and enhance energy levels. From North Africa, millet is often thought of as food "for the birds."

BUCKWHEAT—Despite the name, buckwheat is not related to wheat; rather, buckwheat comes from the fruit of the buckwheat plant. Buckwheat is rich in zinc, which helps prevent a weak immune system and regulate blood sugar, as well as B vitamins. Traditionally, buckwheat is used in pancakes and noodles.

TEFF—This is an ancient grain from Ethiopia, where it is still a staple of the country's diet. Traditionally, teff flour was used to make a fermented pancake. This nutritional powerhouse is high in iron, protein, calcium, and fiber. Iron is essential to delivering oxygen throughout the body and increasing energy levels.

quinoa lentil pilaf
with roasted cauliflower, pistachios + cranberries

vegan, gluten-free

This dish screams fall. It's loaded with warming ingredients that combine for a totally satisfying, hearty dish. Lentils help to increase the protein content of this vegetarian meal.

1 head cauliflower
2 tbsp olive oil
Himalayan sea salt
3 cloves garlic, minced
2 cups cooked quinoa
1 cup cooked black lentils
1/3 cup cranberries
1/3 cup pistachios

Preheat oven to 425°F. Cut cauliflower into bite-sized pieces and toss with 1 tbsp olive oil and sea salt. Place on a parchment-lined baking sheet and roast in the oven for 25 minutes. In a large skillet, heat 1 tbsp of olive oil over medium heat. Add garlic and sauté until fragrant. Add roasted cauliflower, quinoa, lentils, cranberries, and pistachios. Sauté for 5 minutes then serve.

spaghetti squash
with tomato, spinach, garlic + pine nuts

. . . .

vegan, gluten-free

It was only a few years ago that I first discovered spaghetti squash. Where has this vege-table been my whole life?! I thought. If you haven't tried spaghetti squash, you must. It's super easy to make and is a fabulous substitute for the more carb-heavy pasta. Spaghetti squash is high in both fiber and vitamin A and low in calories. . . . You and your waistline will thank me.

1 spaghetti squash
2 tbsp olive oil
3 cloves garlic, minced
2 pints grape tomatoes
4 cups of spinach
toasted pine nuts, optional
Parmesan cheese, optional
Himalayan sea salt, to taste

Preheat oven to 400°F. Cut squash in half lengthwise and discard seeds. Place on a parchment-lined baking sheet, cut-side down, and roast for 30–45 minutes. On another parchment-lined baking sheet, spread tomatoes and drizzle with 1 tbsp olive oil. Roast for 15–20 minutes. When squash is finished cooking, allow to cool then, using a fork, scrape the squash to get long spaghetti-like strands. In a large sauté pan, heat olive oil over medium heat, add garlic, and stir until fragrant. Turn down heat to low and add to-matoes, spinach, and squash and continue to sauté 3–5 minutes. Season with Himalayan sea salt to taste. Serve with pine nuts and Parmesan cheese on top.

tip: instead of throwing away the squash seeds, you can roast them like pumpkin seeds for a salty snack!

spaghetti squash
with roasted broccoli

. . . .

vegetarian, gluten-free

A dish found at the restaurant True Food Kitchen inspires this version of spaghetti squash. True Food Kitchen was started by one of my favorite integrative doctors, Dr. Weill. I first heard Dr. Weill speak while attending the Institute of Integrative Nutrition in NYC. I loved his perspective on an anti-inflammatory diet and have certainly been inspired by his knowledge.

1 spaghetti squash
2 heads of broccoli, cut into florets
2 cups tomato sauce
8-oz ball of fresh mozzarella
2 tbsp basil, chiffonade

Preheat oven to 400°F. Cut squash in half lengthwise and discard seeds. Place on a parchment-lined baking sheet, cut-side down, and roast for 30–45 minutes. On another parchment-lined baking sheet, spread broccoli and drizzle with 1 tbsp olive oil. Roast for 15–20 minutes. When squash is finished cooking, allow to cool then using a fork, scrape the squash to get long spaghetti-like strands. In a cast-iron skillet, combine squash, broccoli, and tomato sauce. Stir to combine and top with slices of fresh mozzarella and basil. Bake for 15 minutes and serve.

veggie quesadilla
with pistachio artichoke pesto

vegetarian, gluten-free

Years ago, when I taught cooking classes, this was a favorite recipe that we made. Feel free to sub any vegetables or pesto combination. And if you have a panini press, the quesadilla turns out even better! Your kids will love these and so will you.

1 butternut squash,
   peeled and cut into ¼" slices
1 head broccoli, cut into florets
1 onion, peeled and sliced
2 tbsp olive oil
1 cup asiago cheese
6 gluten-free tortillas

Pistachio Artichoke Pesto:
¼ cup unsalted pistachios
2 cloves garlic
1 cup basil
1 cup artichoke hearts
   (canned, rinsed, and drained)
½ lemon, juiced
¼ cup olive oil
Himalayan sea salt, to taste

Preheat oven to 425°F. Toss squash, broccoli, and onion with 1 tbsp olive oil. Line a roasting pan with parchment paper. Place vegetables in roasting pan and put in the oven for 25 minutes. Meanwhile, make pistachio artichoke pesto. In a food processor, combine all pesto ingredients and blend until desired consistency. When vegetables are done, take out of the oven. Lay tortilla on a flat, dry surface. Spread 1 tbsp of pesto on half the tortilla. Layer with vegetables, sprinkle with cheese, and fold in half. Heat a large skillet to medium heat. Add remaining 1 tbsp olive oil. Place folded quesadilla in skillet and cook for 3–5 minutes per side.

skillet-baked penne
with swiss chard, eggplant + burrata

....

vegetarian, gluten-free

While I'm a huge advocate for non-cow milk cheese, every once in a while I allow myself to indulge. It's the 80/20 Rule, remember? Burrata is mozzarella's better half. Rich, creamy, and indulgent, this cheese is hands down scrumptious. Here, I use it to top this skillet-baked pasta dish. Feel free to sub any veggies for a satisfying, comforting dish.

2 tbsp olive oil
2 cloves garlic, minced
1 graffiti eggplant, diced into 2" pieces
2 cups Swiss chard, cut into 1" ribbons
2 cups cooked gluten-free penne pasta
1½ cups arrabbiata tomato sauce
8 oz burrata cheese

In a cast-iron skillet over medium heat, add olive oil and garlic. Sauté garlic until fragrant, 2–3 minutes. Add eggplant and cook for 5–7 minutes. Add Swiss chard, pasta, and sauce. Stir to combine until Swiss chard is wilted. Top with sliced burrata cheese and place in the oven to bake for 15 minutes.

crispy brussels sprouts, kale + mushroom tacos
with pineapple guacamole

vegan, gluten-free

When I lived in NYC, there was an amazing taqueria in the west village that served the most innovative tacos, salsa, and margaritas. This recipe is inspired by my many restaurant visits and festive nights spent at Empellon Taqueria.

2 tbsp coconut oil
2 cloves garlic, minced
1 cup chopped onions
2 cups mushrooms
4 oz Brussels sprouts, shredded
1 bunch of kale, de-stemmed and chopped
1 lime
1 tsp chili powder
½ tsp cumin
1 (15-oz) can refried vegetarian beans
corn tortillas

Pineapple Guacamole:
2 avocados
2 cloves garlic, minced
¼ cup cilantro, chopped
1 tbsp olive oil
Himalayan sea salt, to taste
1 lime, juiced
½ lemon, juiced
1 tbsp adobo sauce
½ cup pineapple, chopped

Heat oil over medium heat. Add garlic and cook until fragrant, about 2 minutes. Stir in onions, mushrooms, Brussels sprouts, and sauté for 7–10 minutes. Add kale, juice of lime, chili powder and cumin. Continue to sauté until kale is wilted, another 3–5 minutes. In a separate skillet, heat refried beans. Meanwhile, make the guacamole. Mash avocado and add garlic, cilantro, olive oil, sea salt, lemon, lime, adobo sauce, and pineapple. Stir to combine. To serve, heat corn tortillas then spread a layer of refried beans on tortillas followed by a spoonful of the vegetable mixture. Top with guacamole and serve.

fettuccine
with asparagus, peas, artichoke + lemon

. . . .

vegan, gluten-free

You know it's spring when asparagus, peas, and artichokes start showing up at the farmers' market and on restaurant menus. I love the combination of all these veggies and think this dish perfectly sums up the season. It's light, extremely flavorful, and allows the vegetables to speak for themselves. Serve with a light, crisp California chardonnay and enjoy the freshness of spring.

8 oz gluten-free fettuccine
3 tbsp olive oil
3 cloves garlic, minced
1 cup asparagus, trimmed,
  cut into 1" pieces
½ cup artichokes, canned
½ cup peas
1 lemon, juiced
Himalayan sea salt
Parmesan cheese, optional

Cook pasta according to packaging. Heat 1 tbsp olive oil in a large sauté pan. Add garlic and cook for 2–3 minutes. Add asparagus, artichokes, and peas. Cook for 5 minutes. Add pasta, 2 tbsp olive oil, and juice of 1 lemon. Serve with a sprinkle of salt and Parmesan cheese (optional).

cauliflower pizza two ways

Pizza can be so heavy and filling at times, yes, even the better-for-you gluten-free kind. So if you are craving a pizza and want a lighter option, this is your answer. Cauliflower pizza is actually quite easy to make and while it doesn't quite taste like a slice off the NYC streets, it can fill that craving for pizza and tastes absolutely delicious.

Cauliflower Crust:

vegetarian, gluten-free

1 head cauliflower, cut into florets
2 eggs
½ cup grated Parmesan cheese
⅛ tsp salt

Preheat oven to 400°F. Place cauliflower florets in a food processor and process until "rice" texture. Place on a parchment-lined baking sheet and bake for 15 minutes. Remove cauliflower from the oven and place into a cheesecloth. Squeeze out all excess liquid from the cauliflower. Once all liquid is extracted from the cauliflower, place in a large bowl and add eggs, Parmesan cheese, and salt. Mix to combine and work into a dough. Transfer dough to a pizza stone or parchment-lined baking sheet and flatten with your hands until a thin, round crust is formed. Bake for 15 minutes then remove from oven and top with desired toppings.

smoked mozzarella, sweet potato, caramelized onions + arugula

. . . .

vegetarian, gluten-free

8 oz smoked mozzarella, sliced into thin rounds
1 sweet potato, roasted and thinly sliced
1 cup caramelized onions
1 cup arugula
½ cup walnuts
2 tbsp olive oil
1 lemon

Cook crust according to directions on page 153. Assemble with sliced mozzarella, roasted sweet potatoes, and caramelized onions. Bake in the oven at 350°F for 8–10 minutes until cheese melts. Meanwhile, in a small bowl, toss arugula with walnuts, olive oil, and juice of 1 lemon. When pizza is finished cooking, serve with arugula on top.

peach, mozzarella + balsamic glaze

. . . .

vegetarian, gluten-free

1 peach, pitted and sliced
8 oz fresh mozzarella, sliced into thin rounds
¼ cup basil, chopped
1 tbsp olive oil
balsamic glaze

Cook crust according to directions on page 153. Brush pizza crust with olive oil and assemble with sliced mozzarella and peaches. Bake in the oven at 350°F for 8–10 minutes until cheese is melted. Serve with basil and drizzle with balsamic glaze.

chickpea, tomato + cauliflower curry
with swiss chard + brown rice

vegan, gluten-free

1 tbsp olive oil
1 clove garlic, minced
1 tbsp ginger, minced
1 yellow onion, chopped
1 head cauliflower, chopped in florets
1 (15-oz) can diced tomatoes
2 tbsp red curry paste
1 (15-oz) can chickpeas, drained
1 (15-oz) can coconut milk
2 cups chopped Swiss chard
1 tsp Himalayan sea salt
cooked brown rice

In a large pan over medium heat, add oil, garlic, ginger, and onion. Sauté until fragrant, 3–5 minutes. Add cauliflower and sauté for 5–7 minutes. Stir in tomatoes, red curry paste, chickpeas, coconut milk, and Swiss chard. Reduce heat to low and simmer for 15 minutes. When fully cooked, season with Himalayan sea salt and serve over brown rice.

pumpkin lentil lasagna

vegan, gluten-free

I love this dish because a) it's vegan, b) it's easy to make, and c) it seems like you slaved over the kitchen stove for hours. The cashew ricotta tastes so much like the real thing, you would hardly know it's not. I served this for Christmas one year (in addition to a prime rib), and it was definitely the favorite of the feast between both vegans and carnivores. Be sure to give yourself extra time to soak the cashews; I like to soak them in water the night before I make the recipe.

Pumpkin Cashew Ricotta:
2 cups raw cashews, soaked for at least 4 hours
2 cups pumpkin purée
1 clove garlic
1 lemon, juiced
1 tsp salt
1 tbsp olive oil

Lasagna:
1 container gluten-free lasagna noodles (I love Capello's)
1 jar marinara sauce
1 cup cooked black lentils
8 oz shredded vegan cheese

Preheat oven to 350°F. Meanwhile, in a high-speed blender, add pumpkin cashew ricotta ingredients. Blend until smooth. Add 1 tbsp of water at a time, if necessary, to reach desired consistency. Set aside. Meanwhile, in lasagna pan, spread a layer of tomato sauce, followed by noodles, pumpkin cashew ricotta, lentils, then sauce. Repeat. Top the lasagna with shredded cheese. Cover lasagna with tin foil and bake for 35–40 minutes or until bubbly.

quinoa veggie fried rice

vegetarian, gluten-free

When I first launched **Purely Elizabeth,** I was constantly sampling our blueberry muffins and chocolate chip cookies in local stores. Five out of seven days a week, I was baking dozens upon dozens of sweet goodies to share. And since it was the beginning, I literally had to sample each and every batch that I made. Whoa, I think my body went into sugar shock. All I craved to balance my body was salt. So this was the solution that I often made for dinner to get me back in balance. Well, at least until the next day of baking.

1 tbsp coconut oil
2 cloves garlic, minced
½ cup onions, chopped
1 large bundle of asparagus,
   trimmed, cut into 1" pieces
½ cup peas
1 cup zucchini, chopped
½ tbsp ginger, minced
2 cups quinoa, cooked
1½ tbsp tamari
2 eggs
Sriracha sauce, optional

Heat coconut oil in a large sauté pan. Add garlic and onion and cook for 2–3 minutes. Add asparagus, peas, zucchini, and ginger. Cook another 5–7 minutes. Add in the quinoa and tamari and cook for 2 minutes. Make a well in the center of the quinoa veggie mixture and add the eggs, scramble. Toss everything together and serve drizzled with Sriracha sauce.

quinoa-crusted eggplant parmesan
over swiss chard + white beans

vegetarian, gluten-free

1 eggplant, sliced in ½" slices
½ cup quinoa flakes
½ cup almond flour
1 egg
2 tbsp olive oil
1 clove garlic, minced
3 cups Swiss chard, chopped
1 (15-oz) can white beans, drained
1 jar tomato sauce
1 (8-oz) ball fresh mozzarella cheese
fresh basil leaves

Preheat oven to 400°F. In a bowl, combine quinoa flakes and almond flour. In a separate bowl, whisk eggs. Dip eggplant into egg mixture then dredge in quinoa mixture, covering to coat. Place on a parchment-lined baking sheet and drizzle with 1 tbsp olive oil. Bake for 15 minutes per side.

Meanwhile, in a large skillet over medium heat, add 1 tbsp olive oil and minced garlic. Sauté garlic until fragrant, about 3–5 minutes. Add Swiss chard, white beans, and 1 cup tomato sauce. Cook for 5–7 minutes. Remove from the heat and pour into a baking dish. Add a layer of eggplant with sliced mozzarella on top, then tomato sauce. Continue to layer ending with mozzarella on top. Cover with foil and bake in the oven for 25 minutes and serve with fresh basil leaves.

hemp pesto pasta
with tomatoes, zucchini + fava beans

vegan, gluten-free

This is the ultimate summer pasta salad dish. My sister requests this every time I make a summer feast. Served warm or cold it's always a crowd pleaser. It's super simple to make and the perfect dish for easy entertaining. I usually end up doubling the hemp seed pesto so that I have extra in my fridge to toss with veggies or a salad the next day. You can even freeze the pesto in ice cube trays so that you have a portioned amount whenever you need it.

8 oz gluten-free pasta
2 tbsp olive oil
2 cloves garlic, minced
1 cup zucchini, chopped
1 cup fava beans, cooked,
** outer skin removed**
1 cup grape tomatoes, halved

Hemp Seed Pesto:
3 cups basil
½ cup walnuts
2 cloves garlic
½ cup extra virgin olive oil
1 lemon, juiced
½ cup hemp seeds
Himalayan sea salt, to taste

Cook pasta according to packaging instructions. Meanwhile, in a food processor, add all the ingredients for the pesto and blend until smooth. In a large sauté pan, warm the olive oil over low heat. Add the garlic and stir until slightly brown and fragrant. Add zucchini and stir 3–5 minutes. Add beans and tomatoes and continue to cook until tomatoes are slightly soft. Strain pasta and put in a large bowl. Toss in veggies and pesto and serve warm or cold.

roasted acorn squash
with millet, swiss chard, cherries + feta

vegetarian, gluten-free

1 acorn squash
2 tbsp coconut oil
2 cloves garlic, minced
1 bunch of Swiss chard, shredded
1 cup millet cooked
¼ cup pecans, chopped
¼ cup cherries
¼ cup feta

Preheat oven to 400°F. Cut squash in half and scoop out seeds. Coat squash with 1 tbsp coconut oil and place on a parchment-lined baking sheet, cut-side down. Roast for 45 minutes. Meanwhile, heat a medium-sized sauté pan to medium-high heat. Add 1 tbsp coconut oil and garlic. Sauté until fragrant, 2–3 minutes. Add Swiss chard and sauté until just wilted, 3–5 minutes. Mix in millet, pecans, cherries, and feta. Stuff squash with filling and serve.

delicata squash macro bowl

vegan, gluten-free

I first learned about a macrobiotic diet while studying at the Institute of Integrative Nutrition. I loved the simplicity of the diet and the idea of getting back to basics. While there are many aspects to this way of living, the actual "diet" focuses on whole foods, consumed in traditional methods. A typical macro bowl includes grains, beans, steamed veggies, sea vegetables, and fermented foods. Whenever I feel like my body needs to be more in balance, a macro bowl is the first thing on my menu.

½ delicata squash,
  sliced and deseeded
1 small bunch of kale,
  destemmed, shredded
½ cup kimchi
1½ cups black rice, cooked
1 cup cooked black beans

Tahini Sriracha Sauce:
¼ cup tahini
¼ cup water
1 tbsp rice vinegar
1 tbsp tamari
½ tbsp coconut sugar
1 clove garlic, minced
Sriracha, to taste

Bring water to a boil. Cover pot and reduce heat to low. Add squash and steam for 5 minutes. Add kale and continue to steam for 5–7 minutes. Remove from stove. Meanwhile, in a small bowl, whisk together the tahini ingredients, adding 1 tsp at a time of Sriracha until desired spiciness. Assemble bowl with kale, squash, kimchi, black rice, and black beans. Drizzle with tahini Sriracha sauce and serve.

6-grain oatmeal
with pesto, sun-dried tomatoes + kale

vegan, gluten-free

Forget sweet oatmeal. Here, we take our 6-grain hot cereal and make it savory!

⅓ cup Purely Elizabeth Ancient 6-Grain Hot Cereal
1¼ cups vegetable broth
1 cup kale, shredded
¼ cup sun-dried tomatoes, diced
2–3 tbsp hemp pesto (page 163)

Cook hot cereal according to package directions. In the last 5 minutes of cooking, add kale, sun-dried tomatoes, and pesto. Stir to combine and continue to simmer. Serve.

squash ravioli
with walnuts + sage

. . . .

vegetarian, gluten-free

1 cup arrowroot starch
¾ cup tapioca flour
½ cup brown rice flour
½ cup almond flour
1 tbsp xanthan gum
4 eggs
1 tbsp olive oil
1 tbsp water

Squash Filling:
1 delicata squash,
  sliced and roasted
¼ cup feta cheese
1 tbsp olive oil
Himalayan sea salt

Sauce:
2 tbsp vegan butter
½ cup walnuts, chopped
¼ cup sage, chopped
2 cloves garlic, minced
salt

In the bowl of a mixer, mix dry ingredients together using the flat beater. Add eggs, water, and olive oil and mix on low speed for 3–4 minutes. Cut the dough into 6 balls. Place the rest of the dough in plastic wrap when not using so dough doesn't grow hard. Using a rolling pin coated in flour, roll each ball into rectangles thin enough to go through pasta roller. Put the dough through the pasta roller and then cut with ravioli cutter.

Meanwhile, in a food processor, add squash, feta, olive oil, and salt. Fill the ravioli, placing a dollop of filling on the pasta, brush water or egg on the edges of the dough, place a layer of pasta on top, and press edges together.

In a large pot, bring water to a boil. Cook the pasta for 3–5 minutes. Drain and set aside. Meanwhile, in a cast-iron skillet, heat butter on medium heat. Add garlic, walnuts, and sage, sauté for 3–5 minutes. Add ravioli and toss to combine. Serve.

fish + poultry.

An eating purely diet consists of mainly plant-based foods. But in moderation, fish and poultry can offer important health benefits, as they are rich in omega-3s and protein. Some of us feel better with animal protein in our diet; some of us do not. Experiment to see how you feel. I like to think of animal protein as a small portion of your overall plate; half your plate should be filled with nutrient-rich leafy greens, a quarter whole grains, and another quarter protein. When choosing animal proteins, quality is key. Look for wild fish over farm-raised fish. Select organic, free-range, hormone- and antibiotic-free meats, eggs, and dairy products whenever possible.

recipes

pistachio-crusted salmon

with garlicky smashed potatoes

. . . .

gluten-free

Salmon is one of my favorite fish to eat. As a Top 10 Superfood, it's loaded with omega-3s (both in EPA and DHA form) that help fight inflammation, make your skin glow, improve cardiovascular health, and make you feel great. This version of salmon is super flavorful, not to mention the addition of garlicky smashed potatoes make it even better. Serve with some sautéed garlic spinach to round out the meal.

Smashed Potatoes:
2 large red bliss potatoes
Himalayan sea salt
2 tbsp olive oil
1 clove garlic, minced
1 tbsp basil, chopped
3 tbsp Parmesan cheese

Salmon:
2 (6-oz) pieces salmon
2 tbsp artichoke pistachio pesto (page 293)
¼ cup pistachios
1 lemon

Preheat oven to 425°F. In a large pot, bring water to a boil. Add a pinch of salt and cleaned potatoes. Let potatoes cook for 20 minutes. When potatoes are done, drain water and let cool. Cut in quarters lengthwise and place on parchment-lined baking sheet. Smash potatoes and drizzle with 1 tbsp of olive oil. Roast in the oven for 15 minutes. When finished cooking, place in bowl and toss with garlic, basil, 1 tbsp oil, and Parmesan cheese.

Meanwhile, spoon 1 tbsp of pesto on top of each piece of salmon, spreading evenly to coat. Coarsely grind the pistachios in a food processor. Sprinkle the pistachios over each piece of salmon. Bake salmon in the oven for 12–15 minutes. Serve with a squeeze of fresh lemon.

pan-seared scallops

over snap peas, kaniwa + pesto

. . . .

gluten-free

2 cups snap peas, trimmed
2 radishes, sliced
1 cup cooked kaniwa
4 tbsp hemp seed pesto (page 163)
2 tbsp olive oil
1 lb scallops

Over high heat, bring a pot of water to boil. Add snap peas and cook 1–2 minutes. Drain and cool in ice water. In a large bowl, toss together snap peas, radishes, kaniwa, and pesto. Set aside. Meanwhile, rinse scallops with cold water and pat completely dry. Heat oil in large skillet over high heat. Add scallops and cook on each side for 2–3 minutes or until golden and cooked through. Serve on top of grains and veggies.

shrimp taco
with chipotle lime slaw

gluten-free

One of the best shrimp tacos I've had was at a roadside stop in Napa. Garlicky and spicy, the tacos hit the spot. I've tried to recreate the recipe here, minus the beautiful vineyard background.

2 tbsp coconut oil
2 cloves garlic, minced
1 lb wild caught shrimp, peeled
   and deveined, tails removed
1 tsp chili powder
1 lime, juiced
Corn tortillas

Chipotle Lime Slaw:
2 cups cabbage, shredded
1 cup unsweetened yogurt
   (dairy or non-dairy)
1 lime, juiced
3 tbsp adobo sauce (or more if you like
   it extra spicy)

Optional Toppings:
guacamole
jalapeños
salsa

In a large skillet over medium heat, warm oil. Add garlic and stir until fragrant, about 2 minutes. Add the shrimp, chili powder, and lime juice and cook for 3–4 minutes until cooked through. Meanwhile, in a large bowl, mix together cabbage, yogurt, lime juice, and adobo sauce. Over a warm tortilla, add shrimp then layer with slaw and optional toppings.

PURELY SCOOP

[PROTEIN]

Of course, the first question anyone on a plant-based diet gets asked is: how will you get enough protein? Well, the answer is simple. Protein comes in many forms—and not just from animals. Here is a handy chart to see where other foods rank on the protein scale.

The following are good protein sources (each serving listed contains approximately 7 grams of protein—some contain a bit more, some contain a bit less).

PROTEIN	SERVING SIZE
ASPARAGUS, BOILED	1½ CUPS
BEANS, COOKED	1½ CUPS
BROCCOLI, STEAMED	1½ CUPS
BRUSSELS SPROUTS, BOILED	1½ CUPS
CACAO, RAW	1½ OZ
CHIA SEEDS	2 TBSP
CHLORELLA	3 PACKS
COLLARD GREENS, BOILED	1½ CUPS
EGG WHITES	3 CUPS
FLAXSEED	2 TBSP
GOJI BERRIES	1½ OZ
HEMP POWDER	1½ TBSP
KALE, BOILED	2 CUPS
LEAN CHICKEN, RED MEAT, OR PORK*	1 OZ-WT
LENTILS, COOKED	½ CUP
MISO	2 OZ
NUTRITIONAL YEAST	1½ TBSP
OATS, WHOLE GRAIN, COOKED	1 CUP
MISO	2 OZ
NUTRITIONAL YEAST	1½ TBSP
OATS, WHOLE GRAIN, COOKED	1 CUP
PEANUT BUTTER	2 TBSP
PEANUTS, RAW	¼ CUP
PUMPKIN SEEDS, RAW	¼ CUP
QUINOA, UNCOOKED	¼ CUP
SALMON, COD, TUNA, OR OTHER COLD-WATER FISH*	1 OZ-WT
SPINACH, BOILED	1½ CUP
SPIRULINA	14 GRAMS
SWISS CHARD, BOILED	2 CUPS
TEMPEH, COOKED	¼ CUP
TOFU, RAW	3 OZ-WT

* A typical serving of meat, chicken, or fish is 3–4 ounces, which is about the size of the palm of your hand.

pan-seared halibut
with pesto gnocchi + brussels sprouts

gluten-free

1 cup Brussels sprouts, shredded
3 tbsp olive oil
2 (6-oz) pieces of halibut
1 cup cooked gnocchi
⅓ cup artichoke pistachio pesto
   (see page 293)

Gnocchi:
2 lbs russet potatoes
1 egg
½ cup potato flour
Himalayan sea salt

Preheat oven to 400°F. Line a baking sheet with parchment paper. Place Brussels sprouts on baking sheet, tossed with 1 tbsp oil and roast for 10 minutes until golden brown. Meanwhile, in a skillet, heat 2 tbsp olive oil over medium heat. Add halibut, skin-side up and cook for 3 minutes. Flip halibut and cook for another 3 minutes. Serve on top of gnocchi with drizzled pesto and Brussels sprouts.

Preheat oven to 450°F. Prick potatoes with a fork and place in the oven for 45 minutes or until a knife can easily pierce the potatoes. When potatoes are finished, take out of the oven and let cool for 5 minutes. Discard skin and mash in a bowl or put potatoes through a potato ricer. Add egg and beat with a fork. Add in flour and combine with hands, creating a dough consistency. On a floured surface, roll out dough into 1" logs. Cut gnocchi into ½" pieces and place on a parchment-lined baking sheet. To cook, boil water and place gnocchi in water, cooking for 1–2 minutes until gnocchi rise to the top. Alternatively, instead of cooking in water, sear gnocchi in a skillet until browned on each side, 1–2 minutes.

miso-glazed cod
with asian vegetable slaw

gluten-free

This dish is a rendition of the miso-glazed black cod at the restaurant Nobu. The first time I ate this entrée, I thought I had died and gone to fish heaven. The miso is so flavorful and the cod simply melts in your mouth. Miso, a fermented food, is great for digestion and soothing inflammation. The trick to making this recipe even more flavorful is to marinate it in the refrigerator for 24 hours.

¼ cup mirin
⅓ cup sake
2 tbsp maple syrup
3 tbsp sweet white miso
2 (6-oz) black cod fillets

In a small bowl, whisk together mirin, sake, maple syrup, and miso. Place cod in a baking dish and slather with miso dressing. Marinate up to 24 hours. Preheat oven to 400°F. Bake for 10 minutes, broil for an additional 2–3 minutes. Serve with Asian Vegetable Slaw.

**Asian Vegetable Slaw
with Almond Ginger Dressing:**

Dressing:
2 tbsp maple syrup
¼ cup olive oil
¼ cup rice vinegar
1 tbsp tamari
1 tsp sesame oil, toasted
1 tbsp almond butter
1 tbsp fresh ginger, minced
1 clove garlic, minced

Slaw:
4 cups cabbage and carrots, shredded
1 red bell pepper, thinly sliced
2 medium scallions, finely sliced
1 baby bok choy, thinly sliced
1 tbsp sesame seeds

Make the dressing by combining all the ingredients in a medium bowl. Whisk until smooth. Set aside. Combine all of the slaw ingredients in a large bowl. Add the dressing and toss well.

miso

PURELY SCOOP
[FERMENTED FOODS]

Foods have the incredible power to heal the body, from healing the gut of digestive issues, clearing up acne and eczema, to ridding the body of cancer. What we put into our body is extremely powerful. Hippocrates, one of the great founders of medicine, famously remarked, "Let food be thy medicine, and medicine be thy food." It is with this statement that societies have been using food to heal the body for centuries.

Fermented foods provide a powerful tool to heal the body. They provide "good bacteria" to the gut, helping ease digestion, enhance immunity, and decrease inflammation in the body. Almost 80 percent of your immune system exists in your gut, so having a healthy digestive system is crucial to your immune system and defending against disease. Fermented foods also provide enzymes that help to better absorb minerals, vitamins, and nutrients.

Fermented foods include miso, tempeh, sauerkraut, kombucha, kimchi, cultured veggie, and fermented milk, such as yogurt and kefir. Besides being great for you, these foods are also quite tasty and should be incorporated in your daily diet! You can find these fermented foods in the refrigerator section of your health-food store.

kimchi

yogurt

shrimp puttanesca
over zucchini pasta

gluten-free

Instead of traditional pasta, here I use zucchini pasta as the base for the puttanesca sauce. If you have a spiralizer, you can create the noodles at home; if not, some health-food stores now carry the option in the produce section. The spiciness of the pasta pairs perfectly with an organic pinot noir. Cheers!

2 tbsp olive oil
2 cloves garlic, minced
1 small yellow onion, chopped
1 (24-oz) can diced tomatoes
2 cups kale, shredded
1 cup artichoke hearts, grilled or canned
½ cup Kalamata olives, pitted
2 tbsp capers
1 tsp red pepper flakes, crushed
1 lb shrimp
4 cups spiralized zucchini noodles
feta

Heat olive oil in a large skillet over medium heat. Add garlic and cook until fragrant, 2–3 minutes. Add onion and cook, stirring until browned 5–7 minutes. Stir in the canned tomatoes, kale, artichokes, olives, capers, and red pepper flakes. Bring to a boil then reduce heat to a simmer and cook for 15 minutes. Add zucchini noodles and shrimp to the sauce and cook for 3–5 minutes or until shrimp is cooked through. Serve with crumbled feta on top.

[PURELY SCOOP: ORGANIC WINE]

There's so much emphasis on eating organic foods, the same thinking should apply to what we are drinking. Organic wines are made from grapes grown without pesticides and other chemical toxins. For a wine to bear the USDA organic seal, it can not contain any added sulfites. To be labeled MADE WITH ORGANIC, the wine can have added sulfites. Which labels to buy? A few great California brands include Frey, Robert Sinskey, Benziger, and Domaine Carneros.

tip: marinate the salmon in the fridge for 24 hours to maximize flavor.

maple-glazed salmon
with stir-fried veggies + cashews

....

gluten-free

I've been making this staple salmon for years, probably since college when I had my first kitchen. Friends and clients who don't even like salmon love this preparation. It's super flavorful and will definitely have your guests asking for more.

¼ cup tamari
3 tbsp maple syrup
3 tbsp sesame oil
2 (8-oz) wild salmon
1 tbsp fresh ginger, thinly sliced
2 cloves garlic, minced
2 scallions, thinly sliced
2 tbsp sesame seeds

Stir-Fried Veggies + Cashews:
1 tbsp coconut oil
1 small yellow onion, chopped
1 cup shiitake mushrooms, sliced
2 heads baby bok choy, chopped
1 tbsp mirin
1 tbsp tamari
½ cup cashews, crushed
sesame seeds

In a large, shallow dish, whisk the tamari with the maple syrup and sesame oil. Add the salmon and turn to coat. Press the ginger and garlic onto both sides of the salmon. Cover and refrigerate for 2 hours, turning the salmon a few times. Preheat oven to 450°F. In an ovenproof dish, cook salmon for 10–12 minutes or until salmon is opaque in the center. Transfer to serving plate and garnish with scallion and sesame seeds, serve with stir-fried veggies.

Heat oil in a large pan over medium heat, add onion and cook for 5 minutes, stirring occasionally. Add shiitakes, bok choy, mirin, and tamari. Cover and cook 3 minutes. Toss in cashews and stir. Serve and garnish with sesame seeds.

parchment-baked halibut with tomatoes, zucchini, garlic + grilled artichokes

. . . .

gluten-free

The first time I made parchment-baked fish, I immediately fell in love. I was taking a cooking class at Whole Foods in NYC and could not believe how simple and flavorful the fish could be with this technique. I hope you feel the same! Feel free to sub in any veggies and fish.

2 tbsp olive oil
2 cloves garlic, minced
1 cup tomatoes, diced
1 medium zucchini,
   cut into thin half moons
2 cups artichoke hearts, chopped
   (grilled are even better)
4 (6-oz) halibut fillets or
   other white fish
Himalayan sea salt
4 pieces parchment paper,
   cut into heart shape
4 tbsp white wine
2 lemons, cut in half

Preheat oven to 425°F. In a skillet over medium heat, add 1 tbsp olive oil and garlic. Sauté 3–5 minutes until fragrant. Add zucchini, tomatoes, and artichoke hearts. Sauté for 5–7 minutes and set aside. Place the fish on one side of the heart-shaped parchment paper. Season the fish with salt. Evenly distribute the vegetables on top of the 4 pieces of fish. Drizzle each fillet with remaining olive oil and white wine.

Fold over the other side of the heart; make small overlapping folds along the edges to seal. Place on a baking tray and then repeat with the remaining ingredients and parchment. Bake for 10–12 minutes. The parchment paper will puff up and brown. Remove from the oven and serve immediately. Serve with a fresh squeeze of lemon.

fettuccine
with grilled chicken + sun-dried tomato almond pesto

gluten-free

I love serving this dish warm or cold. The longer it sits, the more flavorful it becomes. It's one of those recipes that you make for a party and are so happy to have leftovers the next day. So be sure to make a big batch! Instead of typical basil pesto, this changes it up with a scrumptious sun-dried tomato almond variety.

2 breasts organic chicken
1 tbsp olive oil
1 lemon, juiced
1 clove garlic, minced
1 tbsp shallot, chopped
8 oz gluten-free fettuccine
basil

Pesto:
⅓ cup almonds
1 cup sun-dried tomatoes
½ cup olive oil
1 clove garlic
½ lemon, juiced

In a large bowl, add chicken, olive oil, lemon juice, garlic, and shallot. Coat the chicken in marinade and allow to sit for at least 30 minutes. Heat a grill to medium heat. Cook marinated chicken for 5–7 minutes per side or until done. Set aside. Meanwhile, cook pasta according to package directions. While pasta is cooking, put all pesto ingredients into a food processor and blend until smooth. Place cooked pasta in a large bowl with sliced chicken and pesto. Toss together and serve with fresh basil on top.

slow cooker chicken enchilada with black beans, mushrooms + swiss chard

....

gluten-free

If you don't have a slow cooker, definitely invest in one. You can pick up a slow cooker/rice maker for about $20 and will definitely be happy with the money spent. I love how chicken tastes after it's cooked for several hours in the slow cooker; moist and falling apart, it melts in your mouth. This chicken and veggie enchilada recipe is super easy to make and full of flavor. If you aren't doing chicken, just sub for more veggies. Some butternut squash in there would be fantastic.

3 breasts organic chicken
2 cans (16-oz) enchilada sauce
1 tbsp coconut oil
1 clove garlic
2 cups mixed mushrooms
4 cups Swiss chard, chopped
1 (15-oz) can black beans, drained
6 gluten-free tortilla wraps
4 oz shredded Mexican blend cheese
  (Organic Valley makes a great option)

In a slow cooker, add chicken and half the enchilada sauce. Cook according to slow cooker directions. When finished cooking, set aside and shred chicken with a fork, keeping sauce. Meanwhile, heat a large skillet over medium heat. Add coconut oil and garlic. Sauté until fragrant. Add mushrooms and cook for 3–5 minutes. Add Swiss chard and black beans, continue to sauté for 5 minutes. Add shredded chicken and reserved sauce. Cook for 2 minutes. Place the veggie/chicken combo in the center of each tortilla. Roll up and place in a baking dish. Pour second half of enchilada sauce all over wrapped tortillas. Sprinkle with cheese. Cover and bake at 350°F for 20 minutes. Uncover and bake 5 minutes or until cheese is slightly browned.

ginger soy tilapia
with steamed bok choy + brown rice

. . . .

gluten-free

When visiting my dad in Florida, we always go to this amazing seafood restaurant that serves some of the freshest, most flavorful fish I've ever had. My favorite dish to get is the fish of the day prepared "Hong Kong Style." This is my version of the exquisite dish—tilapia in a broth of scallions, ginger, tamari, and sesame.

2 cloves garlic, minced
2 tbsp fresh ginger, sliced
2 (6-oz) tilapia
2 baby bok choy, cut lengthwise in quarters
4 tbsp tamari
2 tbsp sesame oil
2 tbsp mirin
1 cup brown rice, cooked
¼ cup scallions, chopped
sesame seeds

In a large saucepan add 1" of water, 1 clove of garlic, minced, and 1 tbsp ginger. Bring to a boil. Add tilapia and bok choy. Cover with lid and steam for 3–5 minutes. Meanwhile, whisk together remaining garlic, ginger, tamari, sesame oil, and mirin. When fish and bok choy are done, assemble plate with brown rice, bok choy, and fish on top. Pour dressing and garnish with scallions and sesame seeds.

pecan-crusted trout
over leek, braised swiss chard + lentils

gluten-free

1 whole trout, head removed,
   filleted and de-boned
2 eggs
½ cup almond flour
1 cup pecans, crushed
1 tbsp olive oil

In a bowl, whisk together eggs and set aside. In two separate bowls, add almond flour and pecans. Dredge the trout in the almond flour, dip into the egg mixture, then dredge in the pecans until the entire fish is coated. In a large sauté pan, add olive oil. Heat to medium high. Place trout skin-side up and panfry for 5–6 minutes or until cooked through.

Lentils and Swiss Chard:

1 tbsp olive oil

2 cloves garlic, minced

1 onion, chopped

½ tsp cumin

¼ tsp coriander

1 cup black lentils

3 cups vegetable stock

2 beets, roasted, chopped

Himalayan Sea Salt

½ cup vegetable broth

1 leek, chopped

1 clove garlic, minced

1 bunch of Swiss chard, stems
   discarded and chopped

In a medium sauté pan, add olive oil, garlic, onion, and spices. Sauté until fragrant, 3–5 minutes. Add lentils and 3 cups stock; bring to a boil. Reduce heat and simmer, 30–40 minutes. Stir in beets and season with salt to taste. Meanwhile, in a separate pan, add vegetable broth. Add chopped leeks and garlic and sauté for 3–5 minutes. Add Swiss chard and sauté for 3–5 minutes or until slightly wilted.

turkey meatballs
with pasta marinara

gluten-free

When I first started racing in triathlons, I'm pretty sure I was more excited for the pre-race dinner than the 4 a.m. wake-up call. My go-to meal was typically a carb heavy pasta with a drool worthy protein-rich bolognese sauce. The combo of the protein and carbs kept me perfectly fueled throughout the race and likely dreaming for more. Here's a cleaned-up version, gluten-free and completely delicious. Heck, if you're feeling adventurous, eat it then wake up and do a triathlon.

1 lb ground organic turkey
1 egg
2 cloves garlic, minced
1 tbsp olive oil
¼ cup Parmesan cheese
2 tbsp chopped basil

Preheat oven to 350°F. In a large bowl, combine turkey, cracked egg, garlic, oil, Parmesan, and basil. Stir to combine. Roll into 1" meatballs. Heat a large skillet over medium heat. Add 1 tbsp olive oil. In batches, cook meatballs until browned, about 2–3 minutes per side. Put in the oven and finish cooking for 15–20 minutes. Serve with pasta marina.

quinoa-crusted chicken
with spicy honey mustard

. . . .

gluten-free

1 lb boneless, skinless organic chicken breasts, cut in strips
½ cup almond flour
¼ cup quinoa flakes
¼ cup shredded coconut
1 egg
1 tbsp olive oil

Spicy Honey Mustard:
⅓ cup honey
¼ cup Dijon mustard
¼ tsp Sriracha

Preheat oven to 375°F. In a bowl, combine almond flour, quinoa flakes, and coconut shreds. In a separate bowl, whisk eggs. Dip chicken into egg mixture then dredge in quinoa mixture, covering to coat. Place on a parchment-lined baking sheet and drizzle with olive oil. Bake for 15–20 minutes then put under the broiler for 1 minute to crisp. Meanwhile, in a small bowl, whisk together honey mustard and Sriracha. Serve chicken with spicy honey mustard sauce.

desserts.

Dessert—my favorite part of the meal. Since I was little, I've always had a sweet tooth. Salty chips never interested me, but baked goods were a different story. Strangely, I never liked chocolate, but I always had my eye on fruit-based desserts. In this chapter, I share with you some of my favorites, all recreated with a healthier twist, subbing better-for-you sugars, oils, and flours. Most of the recipes are fresh and light, leaving you feeling satisfied, not sluggish.

recipes

raw raspberry lemon cheesecake

. . . .

vegan, gluten-free

When I was 15, I discovered the Cheesecake Factory with my best friends from camp. I can still taste that life-altering first bite of cookie dough cheesecake. I literally thought I had found dessert nirvana. God knows what was in that cheesecake that made it weigh a pound. I don't think I want to know. Here's a much lighter and healthier option, which is actually raw. The cashews provide a totally rich taste; you'll be surprised how amazing a raw cheesecake can be.

Crust:
1 cup pecans
1 cup dates, pitted
½ tbsp coconut oil
1 tbsp chia seeds
½ tsp cinnamon

Filling:
2 cups cashews
1 tsp vanilla
2 lemons, juiced
⅓ cup coconut oil
⅓ cup coconut sugar
2 cups raspberries
¼ cup maple syrup

In a food processor, blend crust ingredients until a crumbly paste is formed (so it can stick together with your hands). Place a piece of parchment paper on top of a pie dish and spoon crust mixture on top of the parchment paper. With your hand, press the mixture into the pie dish. In a high-speed blender, blend cashews, vanilla, lemon juice, coconut oil, and coconut sugar. Pour half the filling on top of crust. With the remaining half, continue to blend with raspberries and maple syrup, leaving a few raspberries to the side for decoration. Pour raspberry filling on top of cashew filling and place in the refrigerator for an hour before serving. When ready to serve, remove the parchment paper and top with raspberries.

poached pears
with coconut whipped cream

. . . .

vegan, gluten-free

I love how simple and beautiful this dessert is. Served with some coconut whipped cream on top, it truly makes for a guilt-free sweet treat. Coconut whipped cream is fantastic and incredibly easy to make. It's the perfect recipe to have in your healthy baking arsenal.

750 ml bottle of red wine, such as zinfandel
¾ cup coconut sugar
1 vanilla bean, split in half lengthwise
1 cinnamon stick
4 Bartlett pears, peeled
orange rind

Coconut Whipped Cream:
1 can of coconut milk
1 tsp vanilla
3 tbsp coconut sugar

In a large pot, add a bottle of wine, sugar, vanilla bean, cinnamon stick, and orange rind. Bring to a simmer. Place pears in pot and simmer for 25 minutes. Meanwhile, make the coconut cream. Open a can of coconut milk and pour out the water. Scoop out the coconut cream and place in a bowl. Add vanilla and coconut sugar and whip on high for 2–3 minutes using a hand mixer. Serve poached pears with a dollop of coconut cream on top.

dates

coconut sugar

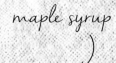
maple syrup

PURELY SCOOP
[SUGAR]

Okay, I must admit it. I love sugar. In a perfect world, I would eat decadent desserts daily. But let's be honest, we all know excess sugar can harm our health. Studies show that too much sugar in the diet can lead to heart disease, diabetes, and cancer, just to name a few. Do you know that the average American consumes more than 150 pounds of sugar every year? Cavemen used to consume between 20 and 30 teaspoons in a lifetime! Sugar is everywhere in our society. Not only in traditional desserts but also in unexpected places like ketchup, breads, and soups. So it's important to watch not only our overall sugar intake but also the sources of sugar. Not all sugars are created equal. There are many sugars on the market that are refined and, once consumed, strip the body of nutrients and make blood sugar soar. My favorite sweeteners to use in cooking and baking, however, are actually nutrient-rich, and some are low glycemic. These include coconut sugar, maple syrup, and dates.

banana bread
with walnuts + chocolate chips

vegetarian, gluten-free

Growing up, my mom always made the most delicious banana bread on the planet. I remember lingering in the kitchen after the bread went in the oven so that I could lick both the spatula and bowl clean. The baked result tastes just as heavenly. When I was in nutrition school, one of the first recipes I wanted to convert to a healthier option was my mom's banana bread. Here, I swap in coconut sugar, coconut oil, and better-for-you flours for healthy banana bread that actually tastes like my mom's. Trust me, it's so good you won't stop with one slice.

Cinnamon sugar (2 tbsp of coconut sugar for every 1 tsp of cinnamon)
1 cup coconut sugar
½ cup almond flour
½ cup millet flour
½ cup brown rice flour
½ tsp cinnamon
1 tsp baking soda
3 very ripe bananas
⅓ cup coconut oil
2 eggs
1 tsp vanilla
⅓ cup walnuts
½ cup chocolate chips

Preheat oven to 350°F. Use an oil spray or coconut oil to grease loaf pan. Sprinkle cinnamon sugar to coat the bottom and sides and set aside. Meanwhile, in a large bowl, stir together the sugar, flours, cinnamon, and baking soda until well combined. In a separate bowl, whisk together the bananas, oil, eggs, and vanilla until smooth. Pour the wet ingredients into the dry and stir until combined. Fold in the walnuts and chocolate chips. Pour into loaf pan and bake for 45–50 minutes.

tip: be sure to use overripe bananas — those that have dark spots on the outer skin.

carrot cake
with cashew cream frosting

vegetarian, gluten-free

It's no doubt that I have always had a huge sweet tooth. This was one of the reasons that propelled me to start **Purely Elizabeth**, after all. I came up empty handed when searching for a better-for-you gluten-free sweet treat. But when I realized what was in vanilla frosting, I knew there had to be an alternative. Cashews are actually the perfect solution for a creamy sweet topping. Be sure to soak the cashews for at least 4 hours to get them smooth and creamy in the vitamix.

¾ cup brown rice flour
²/₃ cup almond flour
¼ cup garbanzo fava flour
¼ cup arrowroot starch
1 tsp Himalayan sea salt
1 tsp baking soda
1 tbsp cinnamon
1 tsp nutmeg
½ cup coconut sugar
3 eggs
¼ cup maple syrup
½ cup olive oil
1½ cups carrots, grated
½ cup golden raisins
½ cup walnuts

Cashew Cream Frosting:
2 cups cashews, preferably soaked for a
   couple hours
1 lemon, juiced
2 tbsp coconut oil
¹/₃ cup maple syrup
1 tsp vanilla

In a large bowl, combine flours, arrowroot, salt, baking soda, cinnamon, nutmeg, and coconut sugar. In a separate bowl, whisk together eggs, maple syrup, and oil. Pour wet ingredients into dry along with carrots, raisins, and walnuts. Stir to combine evenly. Pour into greased muffin tin or cake pans. Bake at 350°F for 30 minutes or until a toothpick comes out clean. Meanwhile, in a high-speed blender, combine cashew cream frosting ingredients. Blend until smooth. Add water as needed until smooth frosting consistency is achieved. Allow to cool before spreading with cashew cream frosting.

peanut butter cup cookies

. . . .

vegetarian, gluten-free

Growing up, whenever we saw my aunt, she always had a fresh tin of Reese's Peanut Butter Cup thumbprint cookies. The salty/sweet combination just melted in your mouth. It's funny because I've never been a big fan of chocolate. In fact, I don't like chocolate at all. But the one exception to that are Reese's Peanut Butter Cups. Since childhood, they have been my favorite candy. So when the company Justin's came out with a healthier option, I was thrilled. Here's my take on my aunt's special treat.

1 cup peanut butter
1 cup coconut sugar
1 egg
1 tsp baking soda
4 Justin's Peanut Butter Cups, cut into quarters

Preheat oven to 350°F. Line a baking sheet with parchment paper. In a mixer, combine peanut butter, sugar, egg, and baking soda. Blend for 2–3 minutes until well combined. Roll into 1" balls. Add a piece of Justin's Peanut Butter Cup on top of each. Bake for 10–12 minutes.

raspberry chia jam thumbprint cookies

. . . .

vegan, gluten-free

My great grandmother always had Pepperidge Farm cookies waiting to greet us. Those cookies are part of one of my earliest food memories. I think it's been decades since I last ate one, but over the years I have never forgotten one of my childhood favorites. My first foray into Whole Foods Market wasn't with **Purely Elizabeth** products but rather with cooking classes I taught. This recipe was a highlight from my Healthy Gluten-Free Baking class.

1 cup Purely Elizabeth Ancient Grain Original Oatmeal
1 cup almond flour
¾ cup millet flour
½ cup olive oil
¼ cup maple syrup
½ cup coconut sugar
3 tbsp chia seeds
½ tsp Himalayan sea salt
raspberry chia jam (page 311)

Preheat oven to 350°F. In a food processor, pulse together oats, almond flour, millet flour, olive oil, maple syrup, coconut sugar, chia, and sea salt. With your hands, roll dough into 1" balls and place on lined cookie sheet. Using your thumb, press into center of ball to create an indentation. Place a dollop of jam in the indentation. Bake in the oven for 15 minutes.

crisps for every season:

Some of my fondest memories of summer include my mom's freshly baked fruit crisps. If there were one type of dessert that I could eat for the rest of my life, this would be it. No chocolate or cake for me. This is an updated, hassle-free version of my mom's recipe, where the fruits can easily be swapped for whatever is in season.

blueberry granola crisp

vegan, gluten-free

3 cups blueberries, fresh or frozen
½ cup coconut sugar
½ lemon, juiced
3 tsp cinnamon
2 tbsp arrowroot powder

Topping:
2 cups of Purely Elizabeth Ancient Grain Granola
2 tbsp of coconut oil or vegan butter

Preheat oven to 350°F. In a large bowl, toss blueberries with the sugar, lemon juice, cinnamon, and arrowroot then spread in a baking dish. In a small bowl, combine the granola with the coconut oil or vegan butter. Sprinkle on the topping and bake for 20 minutes, or until the topping is golden and the filling is bubbling. Serve with coconut-based ice cream.

[PURELY SCOOP: ICE CREAM]

Nothing makes a fruit crisp better than a little à la mode action. Skip the dairy-filled ice creams and instead grab one made with a coconut or cashew milk base. Trust me, your body will thank you. Some of my favorite brands include SoDelicious, Steve's, and Luna and Larry's Coconut Bliss. But remember, it's all about balance, so if you're going to go for dairy, pick a brand that uses high-quality grass-fed milk, like Jeni's. Their Brambleberry Crisp is life changing.

skillet-baked apple cranberry crisp

vegan, gluten-free

2 gala apples, cut into thin slices
1 cup cranberries
2 tbsp lemon juice
¼ cup coconut sugar

Topping:
¼ cup coconut sugar
¾ cup Purely Elizabeth Ancient Grain Original Oatmeal
1 oz vegan butter

Preheat oven to 350°F. Meanwhile, heat a cast-iron skillet over medium heat. Add sliced apples, cranberries, lemon juice, and coconut sugar. Stir and cook for 5–7 minutes. In a bowl, combine topping ingredients. Stir to combine into clumpy pieces. Pour over apple and cranberry mixture and place in the oven for 20 minutes. Serve with coconut milk ice cream on top.

pear, walnut
+ ginger crisp

....

vegan, gluten-free

Pear, walnut, and ginger come together beautifully in this winter version of a fruit crisp. Serve warm with some ice cream, cuddle by the fire, and enjoy a perfect winter's eve.

4 Bartlett pears, sliced
1 tbsp ginger, minced
1 lemon, juiced
⅓ cup coconut sugar

Topping:
1 cup Purely Elizabeth Ancient Grain Original Oatmeal
½ cup walnuts, chopped
⅓ cup coconut sugar
5 tbsp coconut oil
¼ cup millet flour

Preheat oven to 350°F. In a bowl, combine pears, ginger, lemon, and coconut sugar. Meanwhile, in a separate bowl, combine topping ingredients. Pour fruit mixture into an 8 x 8 pan and sprinkle topping evenly. Bake for 30 minutes or until top is browned and fruit is bubbling. Serve with ice cream on top!

strawberry rhubarb crumble

. . . .

vegan, gluten-free

3 cups strawberries, sliced
1 cup rhubarb, sliced
lemon zest
½ lemon, juiced
⅔ cup coconut sugar

Topping:
¾ cup almond meal
½ cup Purely Elizabeth Ancient Grain Original Oatmeal
8 tbsp vegan butter
1 tsp cinnamon
½ cup coconut sugar

Preheat oven to 350°F. In a bowl, combine strawberries, rhubarb, lemon zest and juice, and coconut sugar. Meanwhile, in a separate bowl, combine topping ingredients. Pour fruit mixture into an 8 x 8 pan and sprinkle topping evenly. Bake for 30 minutes or until top is browned and fruit is bubbling. Serve with ice cream on top!

tip: the crust is the perfect base for any raw tart, from chocolate to fruit.

raw pumpkin pie

. . . .

vegan, gluten-free

We all know that Thanksgiving can be one of the heaviest eating days of the year. So why not lighten things up with this delicious raw pumpkin pie. I've never fully followed a raw foods diet, but when it came to learning about raw desserts, I was immediately hooked. There is so much flavor and sweetness in nuts and seeds that sometimes you don't even need the baked alternatives. Use three-inch diameter tartlets for this recipe.

Tart Crust:
2 cup of pecans
1 cup of pitted dates
2 tsp cinnamon
4 tsp coconut oil

Filling:
1 (15-oz) can organic pumpkin purée
⅓ cup coconut sugar
½ cup walnuts
2 tsp pumpkin pie spice

In a food processor, blend crust ingredients until a crumbly paste is formed (so it can stick together with your hands). Place a piece of parchment paper on top of each tartlet. Spoon ¼ of the crust mixture on top of the parchment paper. With your hand, press the mixture into the mold. Repeat with the remaining 3 tartlets. In a food processor, blend filling ingredients until smooth. Pour ¼ of the filling into each crust. Refrigerate for 1 hour to allow the crust to firm and hold. When ready to serve, remove the parchment paper and enjoy.

raw key lime pie

· ·

vegan, gluten-free

Key lime pie is the perfect summertime dessert. This raw version is guilt free, yet totally decadent. Instead of condensed milk, sugar, and other bad-for-you ingredients, avocados are used for the pie filling. Don't worry, no one will ever know.

Tart Crust:
2 cups walnuts
1 cup pitted dates
1 tbsp coconut oil
1 tsp cinnamon

Filling:
2 avocados
½ cup key lime juice
½ cup coconut sugar
¼ cup coconut oil

In a food processor, blend crust ingredients until a crumbly paste is formed (so it can stick together with your hands). With your hand, press the mixture into pie pan. In a food processor, blend filling ingredients. Pour filling into crust. Refrigerate for 1 hour to allow the crust to firm and hold.

tip: stock up on fresh berries
while they are in season.
freeze whatever you don't eat
so you have fresh berries at
your fingertips year-round.

blueberry crumb bar

vegan, gluten-free

I think I love this crumb bar so much because it basically tastes like a crisp but in another form. The filling is so delicious, I like to double the recipe, reserving half of it to use as a jam.

Crumb and Crust:
3 cups Purely Elizabeth Ancient Grain
   Original Oatmeal
½ cup brown rice flour
½ cup almond flour
1 cup coconut sugar
1 tsp baking soda
1 tsp salt
1 tsp cinnamon
1 cup vegan butter, melted
1 cup applesauce, unsweetened

Filling:
3 cups blueberries (fresh or frozen)
1 lemon, juiced
2 tbsp arrowroot powder
½ cup coconut sugar

Preheat to 350°F. Line an 8 x 8 square baking pan with parchment paper. In a large bowl, mix oats, flours, sugar, baking soda, salt, and cinnamon. Add melted butter and applesauce and stir until mixed. Reserve ½ cup crumb mixture for topping; press remaining mixture firmly into the bottom of the baking pan.

Prepare Filling: In a small saucepan, combine blueberries, lemon juice, arrowroot, and sugar. Turn heat to medium and cook, stirring often, until mixture begins to thicken slightly. Remove from heat and pour over crust. Crumble reserved mixture over top. Bake 30 minutes until top is browned. Chill for an hour before cutting.

blackberry mint prosecco pops

. . . .

vegan, gluten-free

1 bottle Prosecco
1 pint blackberries
½ cup chopped mint
1 lime, juiced

Combine all ingredients in a large pitcher and pour into popsicle molds, put on cover, and stick in freezer for about 20 minutes. After the mold has had a little time to set, insert popsicle sticks, being careful not to shove them all the way down (this will make them easier to enjoy when done). Freeze until firm.

key lime pie pops

....

vegetarian, gluten-free

7 key limes, juiced
½ cup coconut sugar
2 cups yogurt
6 oz gluten-free graham crackers

Combine lime juice, sugar, and yogurt in a high-speed blender and blend until smooth. Add in graham crackers and pulse until coarse but still chunky. Pour into popsicle molds, put on cover, and stick in freezer for about 20 minutes. After the mold has had a little time to set, insert popsicle sticks, being careful not to shove them all the way down (this will make them easier to enjoy when done). Freeze until firm.

mango chili coconut pops

vegan, gluten-free

1 cup mango
1 cup coconut milk
¼ cup coconut sugar
chili powder

Combine mango, coconut milk, and sugar in a high-powered blender and blend until smooth. Pour into popsicle molds, put on cover, and stick in freezer for about 20 minutes. After the mold has had a little time to set, insert popsicle sticks, being careful not to shove them all the way down (this will make them easier to enjoy when done). Freeze until firm. Before serving, dip the tips into chili powder.

apple pie

. . . .

vegetarian, gluten-free

Crust:
1½ cups almond meal
¾ cup brown rice flour
½ cup tapioca flour
¼ cup arrowroot powder
¼ cup coconut sugar
½ tsp sea salt
1 egg
½ cup vegan butter + 1tbsp for brushing pie crust

Filling:
1 lemon, juiced
1 tbsp arrowroot powder
¼ cup coconut sugar
1¼ tsp ground cinnamon
¼ cup rosé
6 cups pink lady apples, peeled, cored, and thinly sliced

Preheat oven to 350°F. In a food processor, combine dry crust ingredients. Pulse a few times. Add vegan butter and pulse until combined and crumbly. Add egg, pulsing to combine to form dough consistency. If necessary, add 1 tsp of water. Separate dough into two balls. On a greased pie pan, press one dough ball evenly to cover pan. Meanwhile, in a large bowl combine pie filling ingredients. Toss to combine and evenly coat apples. Pour apples into pie pan. Place the second dough ball on top of parchment paper and cover with Saran wrap. Roll out dough into ¼" thickness. Cut into 1" strips and place on top of apples to create lattice top crust. Brush lattice top crust with remaining 1 tbsp of vegan butter. Bake in the oven for 40 minutes. Serve warm with coconut milk ice cream.

warm baked apple
with oatmeal crumble

. . . .

vegan, gluten-free

6 gala apples
⅔ cup Purely Elizabeth Ancient Grain Original Oatmeal
⅔ cup coconut sugar
¼ cup coconut oil
½ tsp cinnamon
1 tsp vanilla extract
2 cups apple cider
ice cream

Preheat oven to 400°F. Core the apples, cutting ⅔ of the way down to remove seeds. In a bowl, combine oatmeal, sugar, oil, cinnamon, and vanilla. Mix thoroughly with a fork until it becomes clumped together. Stuff the mixture inside each apple. If there is mixture left over, reserve. Place apples in a large baking dish. Pour apple cider in the bottom of the pan, then bake for about 45 minutes. After 30 minutes, take apples out and spoon the cider over the top of each apple. Sprinkle with additional cinnamon if desired. If you have leftover oat mixture, add more to each apple. Place back in the oven for 10–15 minutes. Serve immediately with ice cream on top.

skillet pumpkin chocolate chip cookies

vegetarian, gluten-free

1 box Purely Elizabeth Chocolate
   Chip Cookie Mix
1 cup pumpkin purée
½ cup olive oil
1 egg
2 tsp pumpkin pie spice
1 tbsp vanilla extract

Preheat oven to 350°F. In a large bowl, mix together cookie mix and remaining ingredients. Whisk to combine. Place cookie dough in a cast-iron skillet and bake for 18–20 minutes. Serve warm with coconut milk ice cream on top.

grilled bananas foster

with raw cinnamon swirl ice cream

vegan, gluten-free

This is such a fun recipe to make on the grill. Everyone in the family will love this.

4 firm bananas, peeled, cut
   lengthwise
⅓ cup coconut sugar
3 tbsp vegan butter
⅓ cup dark rum
raw cinnamon swirl ice cream

Preheat grill to medium high. Once heated, place bananas on oiled grill. Sear for 4–6 minutes then flip and repeat. Remove bananas from the grill and set aside. Meanwhile, in a large sauté pan over low heat, combine coconut sugar and vegan butter. Stir until sugar dissolves. Add rum, and if sauce is hot enough, it will flame on its own. Otherwise, tilt pan away from you until it catches. Continue cooking until flame dies out. Add bananas and cook 1–2 minutes or until heated through. Serve with a scoop of raw cinnamon swirl ice cream.

Raw Cinnamon Swirl Ice Cream:
1 cup of raw cashews (soaked for 24 hours)
1 tbsp vanilla extract
½ cup almond milk
½ cup coconut oil
½ cup maple syrup
1 cup water
Himalayan sea salt

Cinnamon Swirl:
3 tbsp maple syrup
1 tsp cinnamon

Blend all ingredients (except cinnamon swirl) in a high-speed blender. Mix until smooth. Pour into ice cream maker or large glass container. In a separate small bowl, combine maple syrup and cinnamon. Pour cinnamon swirl into ice cream mixture and stir. If using ice cream maker, follow manufacturer's instructions for freezing. Otherwise keep the container in the freezer with lid on, occasionally stirring until frozen.

pumpkin spice donut holes

vegan, gluten-free

½ cup millet flour
½ cup brown rice flour
4 tbsp almond flour
2 tsp baking powder
½ tsp salt
½ tsp cinnamon
½ tsp nutmeg
½ tsp allspice
⅛ tsp ground cloves
½ cup coconut sugar
⅛ cup coconut oil
1 chia egg (1 tbsp chia seeds,
   3 tbsp water)
1 tsp vanilla extract
1 cup pumpkin purée

For the coating:
2 tbsp coconut oil melted
1½ tbsp cinnamon
3 tbsp coconut sugar

Preheat oven to 350°F. Spray a mini muffin tin (or regular muffin tin) with nonstick spray. Set aside. In a bowl, combine flours, spices, baking powder, salt, and sugar. Set aside. In a small bowl, whisk together 1 tbsp of chia seeds with 3 tbsp of water. Set aside for 5 minutes to allow the chia seeds to become gelatinous. In the dry ingredient bowl, add coconut oil, vanilla extract, pumpkin purée, and chia egg. Beat until well combined. Roll into tablespoon-sized balls and place into individual muffin tins. Bake for 15 minutes. Let cool. Melt coconut oil for coating and place in a bowl. In a separate bowl, combine coconut sugar and cinnamon for coating. Dip each donut hole into coconut oil then roll in cinnamon and coconut sugar mixture.

[PURELY SCOOP: CHIA EGG]

Trying to avoid eggs? In most baked good recipes, you can swap out an egg with a chia egg. Just whisk together 1 tbsp of water with 3 tbsp of chia seeds and let sit for 5–10 minutes until a gelatinous consistency is obtained. Voila, you can now use the chia egg as you would a regular egg. Do note, however, a chia egg won't work in all recipes, especially those calling for more the two eggs.

peanut butter brownie sundae

....

vegetarian, gluten-free

Eating purely is all about adding nutrient-rich ingredients to your meals. So instead of a bad-for-you brownie, try swapping in some black beans to add a nutritional punch. Seriously, it may sound weird and kind of gross, but honestly you and your guests will never know!

1 (15-oz) can black beans, drained
½ cup coconut oil
⅔ cup raw cacao
1 egg
¼ cup coconut sugar
1 tbsp vanilla
1 tsp baking powder
1 cup chocolate chips
½ cup peanut butter
non-dairy ice cream

Preheat oven to 350°F. Combine black beans, oil, cacao, egg, sugar, vanilla, and baking powder in a food processor. Blend until smooth. Pour into a bowl and fold in chocolate chips. Pour into greased 8 x 8 pan. In a small bowl, heat peanut butter in microwave for 45 seconds. Pour peanut butter into raw brownie mixture and swirl to combine. Bake for 15–20 minutes. Serve warm with ice cream.

linzer heart cookies

vegan, gluten-free

1 cup brown rice flour
4 tbsp hazelnut flour
4 tbsp coconut sugar
½ tsp baking powder
½ tsp ground cinnamon
⅛ tsp Himalayan sea salt
½ tsp vanilla extract
4 tbsp vegan butter
¼ cup jam (see our favorite on page 311)

Preheat oven to 350°F. Combine dry ingredients in a bowl. Add melted butter and vanilla and stir to combine evenly. Place half the dough in between 2 sheets of parchment paper and roll out to ¼" thickness. Remove the top piece of parchment and cut into desired shapes. Continue until all dough is used. On a parchment lined baking sheet, place cookies and bake for 10–12 minutes. When cooled, make the sandwiches by spreading jam on the bottom cookie.

lemon squares

....

vegetarian, gluten-free

Crust:
1½ cups almond meal
¾ cup brown rice flour
½ cup tapioca flour
¼ cup arrowroot powder
¼ cup coconut sugar
½ tsp Himalayan sea salt
½ cup vegan butter
1 egg

Filling:
4 eggs
1 cup lemon juice
½ cup maple syrup
2 tbsp lemon zest
2 tbsp arrowroot powder

Topping:
powdered sugar

Preheat oven to 350°F. In a food processor, combine dry crust ingredients. Pulse a few times. Add vegan butter and pulse until combined and crumbly. Add egg, pulsing to combine to form dough consistency. If necessary, add 1 tsp of water. Grease an 8 x 8 pan with oil or vegan butter and press dough evenly into the baking dish. Bake for 15-20 minutes, until edges brown. Meanwhile, in a large bowl, whisk together filling ingredients. Once crust is finished cooking, take it out of the oven. Pour filling ingredients on crust and return it to the oven for another 15-20 until edges brown and filling is set. Allow to cool, then refrigerate to set. Top with powdered sugar and cut into squares to serve.

CHAPTER 9

drinks.

The 80/20 Rule allows for balance, which means pairing a smoothie in the morning with the occasional cocktail in the evening. This chapter features drinks that can be savored and sipped at a party or consumed for a much-needed detox. From a make-your-own mojito bar to the satisfying richness of a kiwi banana smoothie, the drinks in this chapter combine a range of flavors to get your day off to a bright start or to top off occasions year-round. The one feature that all the fresh cocktails and smoothies have in common in this section is they use the freshest ingredients at the market.

recipes

spring thyme lemonade

. . . .

vegan, gluten-free

1 oz vodka
1 lemon, juiced
1 oz St. Germain or simple syrup
1 sprig of thyme
club soda
ice

In a cocktail shaker add vodka, lemon juice, and St. Germain. Shake to combine. Pour into an ice-filled glass and top with club soda and a sprig of thyme.

fresh peach strawberry bellini

. . . .

vegan, gluten-free

4 ripe peaches, seeds removed
   and quartered
2 cups strawberries
⅓ cup water
1 (750-ml) bottle Prosecco

In a high-speed blender, blend the peaches, strawberries, and water until smooth. Chill the fruit purée for a couple of hours or until ready to use. To prepare the bellini, pour the purée into champagne flutes and gently top off with Prosecco for a 1:1 ratio.

watermelon blackberry margarita

vegan, gluten-free

This margarita is perfect in the heat of the summer. Score some fresh berries from the farmers' market, sit back, and enjoy.

2 cups blackberries
4 cups watermelon
2 limes, juiced
4 oz tequila
salt

Put all ingredients in a high-speed blender and blend until smooth. Serve on ice with a salted rim.

strawberry mint sangria

. . . .

vegan, gluten-free

1 bottle white wine, such as a pinot grigio
2 cups sparkling water
1 pint strawberries, sliced
½ cup fresh mint
ice

Add all ingredients to a pitcher, leaving aside 3–4 strawberries and 3–4 sprigs of fresh mint per glass. Place pitcher in the fridge and chill. When ready to serve, muddle strawberries and mint and pour over ice.

kombucha martini

. . . .

vegan, gluten-free

I first had a kombucha cocktail at a Whole Foods party in NYC. The taste was out of this world, but even more so I loved that there were some health benefits to the drink. Alcohol plus fermented kombucha to help with digestion and immunity? Yes, please! Try making this with your favorite local kombucha. There are so many amazing ones out there.

1 part vodka, such as Tito's Handmade Vodka (gluten-free)
2 parts ginger kombucha
1 lemon
ice

Combine vodka and kombucha. Shake mixture over ice. Pour into glass and serve with a twist of lemon.

roasted pineapple habanero margarita

. . . .

vegan, gluten-free

Anyone who knows me knows that I love spice and heat . . . particularly in a cocktail. The hot habanero and roasted pineapple pair perfectly to create this refreshing libation. This is always served on homemade Mexican night.

1 bottle tequila
3 habanero peppers
1 pineapple
3 limes, juiced
salt

Cut habaneros in strips, discarding the seeds and stem. Put habaneros in the bottle of tequila and let sit for 24 hours. Drain tequila and reserve. Meanwhile, preheat oven to 425°F. Cut pineapple into ½" round slices. Place on a parchment lined baking sheet and roast for 15 minutes. When pineapples are done and cooled, place in a high-speed blender with tequila and lime juice. Blend until smooth. Serve on ice with a salted rim.

purely dirty cocktail

....

vegan, gluten-free

1 part vodka, such as Tito's Handmade Vodka
2 parts beet-based juice, such as Blueprint or Suja ice

Combine vodka and juice. Shake mixture over ice. Pour into glass and serve. Kill two birds with one stone.

spiked apple cider martini

....

vegan, gluten-free

Whenever I smell cider, it instantly transports me back to my high school days, sitting outside of Starbucks with my best friend drinking warm apple cider. The aroma was intoxicating and the taste pretty darn delicious. It actually took me 25 years to eventually try it spiked. What was I missing all these years? This recipe is super simple, but if you make your own spiced cider, it smells and tastes that much better.

lemon
coconut sugar
1 part caramel vodka
3 parts spiced apple cider
apple, sliced

Moisten the rim of a martini glass with lemon. Pour coconut sugar on a plate and dip the glass into coconut sugar, lining the rim all the way around. In a cocktail shaker, add ice and 1 part vodka to 3 parts apple cider. Shake to combine. Pour into martini glass and garnish with sliced apple.

mojitos three ways:

There's something about a mojito that instantly makes a party fun. And setting up a make-your-own mojito bar is even better. Below is a basic recipe to follow. Mix and match fruits and herbs for different seasonal flavor combinations.

blueberry ginger, strawberry basil, grilled pineapple rosemary

vegan, gluten-free

1 oz lime juice
1 tsp coconut sugar or St. Germain Elderflower Liqueur
  (for a sweetener)
fresh fruit: blueberries, strawberries, grilled pineapple
  (about ⅓ cup fruit per drink)
herbs: mint, basil, rosemary
2 oz light or silver rum
ice
club soda

In a small glass, muddle lime juice with ½–1 tsp coconut sugar or Elderflower Liqueur. Add the mint leaves, fresh fruit, and herbs of your choice, muddling them and mushing them against the side of the glass. Fill glass ⅔ with ice and pour in the rum. Top with club soda.

cherry sangria

....

vegan, gluten-free

When cherries hit the farmers' market, you know summer has arrived. Their season always seems to be short, but when you get a ripe cherry, nothing compares. Cherries are loaded with antioxidants and anti-inflammatory properties, rich in potassium and vitamin C.

1 bottle red wine, such as zinfandel
1 bottle sparkling rose
1 cup cherries, halved
ice

Add all ingredients to a pitcher and place in the fridge to chill. When ready to serve, scoop some fruit in each glass and pour over ice.

champagne, vodka + st. germain
with pomegranate

....

vegan, gluten-free

1 part vodka
1 part St. Germain
3 parts champagne
ice
pomegranates

In a cocktail shaker add vodka, St. Germain, and ice. Shake to combine. Pour into a glass and top with champagne and pomegranates.

clementine cocktail

....

vegan, gluten-free

2 clementines , juiced
½ lemon, juiced
1½ oz vodka
sprig of rosemary

Fill your glass with ice, and then
add juices and vodka. Stir. Garnish
with rosemary sprig.

blueberry sparkler

....

vegan, gluten-free

1 bottle champagne
⅓ part St. Germain
1 pint blueberries
lemon

Muddle 4–5 blueberries per
glass. Set aside. Stir Champagne,
St. Germain, and remainder of
blueberries in a tall carafe. Soak
for approximately 15 minutes.
Serve in an ice-filled muddled
blueberry glass with a twist of
lemon. Enjoy!

green goddess smoothie

....

vegan, gluten-free

2 cups kale
½ cup pineapple, chopped
1 tbsp fresh ginger, minced
1 apple, cored and chopped
2 sprigs mint leaves
½ cup water
1 cup ice

Blend all ingredients together in high-speed blender.

kiwi, banana + swiss chard smoothie

....

vegan, gluten-free

1 banana
2 kiwi
1 cup Swiss chard
½ cup almond milk
½ blood orange
1 cup ice
1 tbsp chia seeds

Blend all ingredients together in high-speed blender.

almond butter banana espresso smoothie

....

vegan, gluten-free

1 shot espresso
1 tbsp almond butter
1 banana
1 cup coconut milk
1 tbsp coconut oil
1 cup ice

Blend all ingredients together in a high-speed blender.

pistachio, cardamom + coconut smoothie

vegan, gluten-free

1 cup coconut milk
1 banana
1 tbsp pistachio butter
½ tsp cinnamon
¼ tsp cardamom
ice

Place all ingredients in a high speed blender and blend until smooth.

antioxidant-rich berry smoothie with granola

vegan, gluten-free

½ cup blueberries
½ cup raspberries
½ cup strawberries
1 tbsp chia seeds
1 tbsp flaxseeds
1 tbsp hemp seeds
1 banana
1 cup almond milk
2 tbsp Purely Elizabeth Ancient Grain Granola

Blend all ingredients together in blender, leaving out granola. Pour into glass and sprinkle granola on top.

CHAPTER 10

brunch.

Brunch is one of my favorite meals of the day. There's something so festive and joyous about brunch. Maybe it's because when you start your day purely, all the rest just falls into place! In this chapter, you'll find favorites like the sweet, moist banana granola-crusted French toast kabobs and the rich flavors of the baked eggs with burrata. Recipes in this chapter range from sweet and savory to vegan and egg-based. All recipes are easy and totally delicious.

recipes

baked eggs
with artichokes, kale, burrata + arrabbiata sauce

. . . .

vegetarian, gluten-free

This recipe is inspired by one of my favorite brunch spots in NYC. I love how effortless this recipe is, yet how beautiful and complex it tastes when it's done. Feel free to sub other greens in place of the kale, like spinach or Swiss chard.

1 tbsp olive oil
1 clove garlic, minced
2 cups lacinato kale, shredded
1 cup artichoke hearts (canned, rinsed and drained)
2 cups arrabbiata tomato sauce
8 oz burrata cheese, sliced
3 eggs

Preheat oven to 350°F. In a cast-iron skillet over medium heat, add olive oil and garlic. Sauté until fragrant, 2–3 minutes. Add kale and sauté for 5 minutes. Add artichoke and sauce and continue to cook for 2 minutes. With a spoon, make 3 indentations in the sauce. One at a time, break the eggs into a small bowl and then slip into each indentation. Evenly place the sliced cheese around the pan. Bake for 25 minutes. Serve.

spring vegetable frittata

. . . .

vegetarian, gluten-free

Frittatas are one of the easiest egg dishes to make if you are having a lot of company over for brunch. This recipe replaces traditional heavy cream with non-dairy milk and loads in veggies for added fiber and nutrients. Don't finish the whole thing? Wrap up the remaining slices and freeze for a quick on-the-go breakfast.

10 organic eggs
¼ cup non-dairy milk, unsweetened
1 pint grape tomatoes, halved
1 cup fresh or frozen peas
1 cup asparagus, trimmed, chopped into 1" pieces
2 oz goat cheese
Sriracha, to taste

Preheat oven to 400°F. In a bowl, whisk together eggs, milk, and vegetables. Pour the mixture into a pie dish. Bake until golden and puffy, about 20 minutes. Take frittata out of the oven and sprinkle goat cheese on top. Return to oven for another 5–10 minutes. Serve in wedges with a dab of Sriracha sauce on top.

savory oatmeal
with poached egg + mushrooms

....

vegetarian, gluten-free

Most of us were brought up to think that oatmeal can only be enjoyed as a sweet breakfast. I was pleased to find out this is not true. There is a whole world of savory oatmeals, and, in fact, they are just as incredibly delicious and satisfying as their sweet counterparts. This may be just the thing to shake up your normal Saturday breakfast routine. The 6 grains in the hot cereal add extra fiber to your morning and keep you feeling full and regular.

⅓ cup **Purely Elizabeth Ancient 6-Grain Hot Cereal**
1¼ cup **vegetable broth**
2 tbsp **olive oil**
2 cloves **garlic, minced**
½ **yellow onion, chopped**
1 cup **mushrooms, chopped**
3 cups **Swiss chard, chopped**
2 sprigs **thyme**
⅓ cup **Parmesan cheese**
truffle oil
2 **eggs**

In a small pot, make hot cereal according to package instructions, substituting broth for water. Meanwhile, in a large skillet over medium heat add olive oil and garlic. Sauté for 2–3 minutes until fragrant. Add onion and continue to sauté for 3 minutes. Add mushrooms, Swiss chard, and thyme and sauté until mushrooms are cooked through about 7 minutes. When hot cereal is cooked, add Parmesan cheese and stir for a creamy consistency. Assemble dish with hot cereal then veggies on top. Drizzle with truffle oil. Add poached or fried egg on top.

breakfast pizza
with egg + cheese

vegetarian, gluten-free

I love the idea of doing things when you're not supposed to. One of my all-time favorite birthdays growing up was a backwards-themed party. For dinner, we ate breakfast. Instead of eating at the table, we ate under the table. You get the point. So to me, there's something so fun about pizza for breakfast. Maybe it's the unexpected; maybe it's just that it's totally sinfully delicious. Whatever it is, I hope you enjoy!

1 gluten-free pizza dough
1 tbsp olive oil
½ cup onion, chopped
1 cup fresh mushrooms, sliced
2 cups fresh baby spinach
2 cups mozzarella cheese, shredded
3–4 eggs

Preheat oven to 400°F. Cook dough according to package directions to allow crust to crisp. Meanwhile, in a large skillet over medium heat, add olive oil and onions and sauté for 3–5 minutes. Add mushrooms and cook for 3 minutes. Add spinach and cook for 2 more minutes. Set aside. Assemble pizza, layering veggies, then mozzarella. Crack the eggs on top and bake for 5 minutes or until cheese melts.

grilled fig flatbread
with blackberries, goat cheese, pistachios + honey

vegetarian, gluten-free

gluten-free pizza dough, such as GF Bistro or Udi's
4 figs, sliced
2 oz goat cheese
½ cup blackberries
¼ cup pistachios
1 tbsp honey

Heat grill to medium-high heat. Cook pizza according to dough directions. Grill figs for 2 minutes a side. When pizza is ready for toppings, spread the goat cheese evenly over your pizza. Sprinkle with blackberries, sliced figs, and pistachios. Drizzle with honey.

grilled veggie sandwich
with artichoke pistachio pesto

vegetarian, gluten-free

I love how fresh and satisfying this sandwich tastes. The artichoke pesto elevates this ordinary veggie sandwich to new heights. Whoever said veggie sandwiches were boring definitely has not experienced this.

gluten-free bread
1 red pepper, cut into quarters lengthwise
2 portobello mushrooms
1 zucchini, sliced lengthwise
1 tbsp olive oil
8 oz fresh mozzarella ball

Artichoke Pistachio Pesto:
¼ cup unsalted pistachios
2 cloves garlic
1 cup basil
1 cup artichoke hearts
  (canned, rinsed and drained)
½ lemon, juiced
¼ cup olive oil
Himalayan sea salt, to taste

Preheat oven to 425°F. On a parchment-lined baking sheet, place pepper, mushrooms, and zucchini. Drizzle with olive oil. Roast for 20–25 minutes. Meanwhile, combine pesto ingredients in a food processor and pulse until almost smooth, leaving some chunks for texture. Add sea salt to taste. Set aside. When vegetables are done, allow to cool. Assemble sandwich by spreading pesto on each slice of bread, then stack a slice of fresh mozzarella, zucchini, red pepper, then mushroom. Top with the other piece of bread. In an olive oil–lined skillet, over medium heat, cook sandwich on each side for 2 minutes then serve.

nut butter + jam banana quesadilla

....

vegan, gluten-free

Forget your classic PB & J. Swap out sugar-laden jelly for one made with nutrient-dense chia seeds and coconut sugar. Instead of sugar-infused peanut butter, look for healthier alternatives like Nuttzo, made with seven organic nuts and seeds. Here, the heat from the pan perfectly melts the nut butter and jelly into a delicious, drool-worthy meal, snack, or even dessert. Everyone in the family will love this, especially your kids.

2 tbsp nut butter
1 gluten-free tortilla
1 banana
2 tbsp raspberry chia jam (page 311)

Spread almond butter on one tortilla. Cut banana into thin slices and place on one half of the tortilla. On the other half, spread jam. Fold tortilla in half. Heat a large sauté pan to medium heat. Place quesadilla on pan and brown on each side about 4 minutes each.

blueberry oatmeal muffins

. . . .

vegetarian, gluten-free

My first **Purely Elizabeth** product was actually a blueberry muffin mix. We have since moved away from the muffin mix category, but still get frequent e-mail requests asking for the mix to come back. So in the meantime, here is a take on the original recipe that I know you will love. Feel free to sub other seasonal fruits for the blueberries. I bet peaches would be amazing.

¾ cup brown rice flour
¾ cup millet flour
½ cup almond flour
⅓ cup Purely Elizabeth Ancient Grain
   Original Oatmeal
2 tbsp chia seeds
¾ cup coconut sugar
2 tsp baking powder
½ tsp baking soda
1 tsp Himalayan sea salt
1 tbsp lemon juice
2 eggs
1 tsp vanilla extract
½ cup olive oil
½ cup unsweetened coconut milk
1½ cups frozen or fresh blueberries

Preheat oven to 350°F. Grease muffin pan with olive oil. In a large bowl, whisk together flours, oatmeal, chia seeds, coconut sugar, baking powder, baking soda, and salt. Add the lemon juice, eggs, vanilla, oil, and milk. Whisk to combine. Fold in blueberries. Spoon the batter into the muffin tin and bake for 20 minutes.

banana pecan-crusted french toast kabobs

vegetarian, gluten-free

If you are looking to impress brunch guests, this is definitely the dish to try. The French toast kabobs look beautiful when served and, more importantly, taste absolutely decadent with the blend of cinnamon, vanilla, pecans, and maple syrup. Fun for everyone in the family to eat, you will be sure to make them again.

4 eggs
½ cup almond milk
2 tsp vanilla
2 tsp cinnamon
6–8 slices gluten-free bread, cut into 1–2"cubes
½ cup almond meal
½ cup pecans, finely chopped
1 tbsp olive oil
1 banana
maple syrup
wooden kabob skewers

In a big mixing bowl, combine eggs, milk, vanilla, and cinnamon. Whisk mixture until well combined. Add bread cubes and evenly coat egg mixture. If possible, allow bread to soak in mixture for an hour. Meanwhile, in a small bowl, combine almond meal and pecans. Take each soaked bread cube and dip into the pecan crumbs, covering evenly. Heat olive oil in a large skillet over medium heat. Place the nut-crusted bread onto the pan and cook for 2–3 minutes a side. Assemble kabobs on skewers, alternating with bread and banana slices. Serve immediately with maple syrup.

tip: kabobs make the perfect party food, easy to eat and beautiful to look at. there are so many fun varieties to make from mini pancakes to meatballs and everything in between.

stuffed berry french toast

vegetarian, gluten-free

Want a decadent yet antioxidant-rich Sunday brunch meal? Then this is the perfect solution. It's so easy; simply soak the bread in the egg and milk mixture overnight. In the morning, simply wake up, heat the oven, and serve with fresh berries.

8 eggs
¾ cup almond milk
1 tsp pure vanilla extract
¼ cup maple syrup
1 tbsp cinnamon
8–10 pieces of gluten-free bread
4 cups fresh or frozen mixed berries

In a large bowl, whisk together eggs, milk, vanilla, maple syrup, and cinnamon. Add bread slices and soak overnight. Preheat oven to 350°F. Lightly grease a pan or soufflé dish. When the bread is all soaked, place half the bread slices into the prepared pan. Top with about ⅔ of the mixed berries. Cover the berries with the rest of the bread then top with the last ⅓ of the berries. Bake for 25 minutes and serve with maple syrup drizzled on top.

baked raspberry skillet oatmeal

....

vegetarian, gluten-free

There are so many wonderful ways to eat oatmeal. Here, I use one my favorite kitchen utensils, the cast-iron skillet. This recipe is quick and easy for a pre-work breakfast. Simply stir all the ingredients together for a few minutes then throw it in the oven while you finish getting dressed. This is oatmeal elevated. Yes, your taste buds will thank you.

1 cup raspberries
1 cup almond milk
1 cup Purely Elizabeth Ancient Grain Original Oatmeal
1 egg
1 tbsp vanilla
1 tsp cinnamon
2 tbsp maple syrup

Preheat oven to 350°F. In a cast-iron skillet over medium heat, add raspberries. Sauté for 2 minutes. Add almond milk, oatmeal, egg, vanilla, cinnamon, and syrup. Stir to combine, 3–5 minutes. Put the skillet in the oven and bake for 12 minutes. Serve with maple syrup drizzled on top.

perfect pancakes

....

vegetarian, gluten-free

Nothing says the weekend more than pancakes on a lazy Sunday morning. I love eating these before a long run in the crisp fall air. These pancakes are loaded with nutrition from the addition of flax, hemp, chia, and almond meal. This breakfast will definitely fuel your morning and not leave you wanting to veg on the couch all day—although, no judgments here if that's what your Sunday needs.

2 eggs
¾ cup non-dairy milk
3 tbsp olive oil
1 cup millet flour
¾ cup almond flour
¼ cup brown rice flour
1 tsp baking soda
1 tsp baking powder
½ tsp Himalayan sea salt
1 tbsp chia seeds
1 tbsp hemp seeds
1 tbsp flaxseeds
¼ cup coconut sugar

Whisk eggs, milk, and 2 tbsp of olive oil in a bowl. Add dry ingredients and gently stir to combine. Let sit for 5 minutes. Heat a nonstick skillet over medium heat and lightly coat surface with remaining olive oil. Spoon ¼ cup of mixture onto skillet. Cook until pancake begins to bubble, about 2 minutes. Flip pancake and cook another 2–3 minutes. Serve with warm maple syrup.

ip: can't finish all the pancakes? they freeze perfectly
nd can quickly be reheated for a quick breakfast.

chickpea salad
with currants, walnuts + celery

. . . .

vegan, gluten-free

Rather than traditional chicken salad, here I swap in chickpeas for chicken and Vegenaise for mayo. Chickpeas are loaded with fiber and protein, while walnuts provide omega-3s. Forget the mayo and sub Vegenaise for a completely vegan lunch option. This is great for making a big batch and storing in the fridge for several days.

1 (15-oz) can chickpeas, drained
2 tbsp vegan mayonnaise
1 tbsp Dijon mustard
1 tsp Himalayan sea salt
½ cup celery, chopped
½ cup dried currants
½ cup of walnuts, chopped
gluten-free bread

In a food processor combine chickpeas, vegan mayo, mustard, and salt. Pulse 3–4 times so that consistency is somewhat chunky. Pour into a bowl and mix in celery, currants, and walnuts. Serve on gluten-free bread.

wild blueberry + ginger oatmeal breakfast bar

....

vegetarian, gluten-free

These bars are so easy to make and freeze really well. Wrap them individually so you can grab them out of the freezer for breakfast on the go or as a snack in your kid's lunch box.

1¼ cup almond milk
1 egg
½ tsp vanilla
½ cup coconut sugar
¼ cup maple syrup
3½ cups Purely Elizabeth Original Ancient Grain Oatmeal
½ tsp ginger
2 cups blueberries

Preheat oven to 350°F. In a large bowl, whisk together milk, egg, vanilla, coconut sugar and maple syrup. Add in oats, ginger, and blueberries. Stir to combine. Pour into a greased 8 x 8 pan and bake for 25 minutes.

chia seed jam three ways:

I always thought that jam must be incredibly hard to make, so I continued to buy store-bought varieties for years. Until one day the raspberries at the Union Square Farmers Market were calling to me to be made into a jam. I'm so happy that they did, because the following tasted like heaven. Not to mention this is definitely the healthiest jam you can find on the market.

raspberry jam

. . . .

vegan, gluten-free

2½ lb raspberries
2 cups coconut sugar
1 lemon, juiced
3 tbsp chia seeds

In a 4-quart pan over low-medium heat, combine raspberries, coconut sugar, lemon juice, and chia seeds. Bring to a boil and cook, stirring often, about 20 minutes. Reduce heat to low and simmer for 1 hour until all juices are released and thickened. Store in the fridge or canning jars.

strawberry balsamic jam

. . . .

vegan, gluten-free

2½ lb strawberries
½ cup coconut sugar
¼ cup balsamic vinegar
1 tbsp chia seeds

In a 4-quart pan over low-medium heat, combine strawberries, coconut sugar, balsamic vinegar, and chia seeds. Simmer for 1 hour until all juices are released and thickened. For a smoother consistency, place in a food processor when cooled. Store in the fridge or canning jars.

peach ginger jam

. . . .

vegan, gluten-free

2 lb peaches,
   cored and cut into slices
½ cup coconut sugar
1 lemon, juiced
1 tbsp ginger, minced
1 tbsp chia seeds

In a 4-quart pan over low-medium heat, combine peaches, coconut sugar, lemon, ginger, and chia seeds. Simmer for 1 hour until all juices are released and thickened. For a smoother consistency, place in a food processor when cooled. Store in the fridge or canning jars.

[PURELY SCOOP: MAKE YOUR OWN PARFAIT BAR]

Have different types of homemade jams, yogurts, and **Purely Elizabeth** granola out for guests to make their own granola parfait—a purely delicious breakfast or brunch treat that is totally fun.

skillet-baked corn bread

....

vegetarian, gluten-free

This corn bread is great with both salty or sweet accompaniments. I love it with jam or served with my favorite veggie chili.

2 cups cornmeal
1 tsp Himalayan sea salt
1 tsp baking soda
1 egg
¼ cup olive oil
1½ cups Greek yogurt
¼ cup coconut sugar

In a large bowl, combine all ingredients. Whisk together until smooth. Pour into a skillet and bake for 25 minutes at 400°F. Serve with peach ginger jam (on page 311) or butter.

overnight oats two ways

We all know that oatmeal is one of the healthiest breakfasts for our hearts. But come summertime, hot oatmeal can sometimes be the last thing we want to put in our bodies. Swap out the stove for the fridge and eat this easy-to-make cold breakfast in the morning.

overnight oats
with blackberries, pistachios, basil + coconut

. . . .

vegan, gluten-free

⅓ cup **Purely Elizabeth Ancient Grain Original Oatmeal**
1 cup **coconut milk**
½ cup **blackberries**
2 tbsp **pistachios**
2 tbsp **coconut flakes**
1 tbsp **basil, chiffonade**
maple syrup

Pour oatmeal and milk into a jar and refrigerate overnight. When ready to serve, top with blackberries, pistachios, coconut flakes, and basil. Drizzle with maple syrup for extra sweetness.

[OTHER DROOL-WORTHY OVERNIGHT OATMEAL COMBINATIONS]

Balsamic Maple Strawberries + Mint
Blueberry, Lemon Zest + Poppy
Banana, Cardamom, Cinnamon + Pistachio
Mango, Lime + Cilantro
Blood Orange, Mint, Pomegranate + Toasted Coconut

overnight oats
with balsamic maple strawberries + mint

....

vegan, gluten-free

½ cup Purely Elizabeth Ancient Grain Original Oatmeal
1 cup coconut milk
1 cup strawberries, sliced
2 tbsp maple syrup
1 tbsp balsamic vinegar
1 tbsp mint, chiffonade

Pour oatmeal and milk into a jar and refrigerate overnight. When ready to serve, heat a small sauté pan over medium heat. Add sliced strawberries, maple syrup, and balsamic vinegar and sauté for 3–5 minutes until strawberries soften. Serve on top of oatmeal with mint.

breakfast tacos
with black beans, zucchini, avocado + sriracha

vegetarian, gluten-free

1 tbsp coconut oil
2 cups diced zucchini/summer squash
½ cup cooked black beans
3 organic eggs
4 corn tortillas
1 avocado, cut into slices
Sriracha sauce
1 lime

In a large skillet over medium heat, add ½ tbsp coconut oil. Add diced zucchini and sauté for 5 minutes. Add black beans and continue to cook for 5 minutes. Set aside. Add the other ½ tbsp coconut oil to coat the pan. Meanwhile, whisk eggs in a small bowl. Pour eggs into pan and scramble, about 2–3 minutes. Assemble tacos with bean/veggie mixture, eggs, sliced avocado, a dollop of Sriracha, and a squeeze of lime.

feta + kale waffle
topped with fried egg + avocado

. . . .

vegetarian, gluten-free

²/₃ cup brown rice flour
¹/₃ buckwheat flour
½ cup oat flour
¹/₃ cup Purely Elizabeth Ancient Grain Original Oatmeal
¼ cup arrowroot flour
1½ tsp baking powder
½ cup olive oil
1¼ cup non-dairy milk, unsweetened
1 tsp apple cider vinegar
1 egg
2 cloves garlic, minced
1 cup shredded kale
4 oz feta, crumbled

Toppings:
eggs
avocado
salsa

In a large bowl, combine dry ingredients. In a separate bowl, whisk together milk and apple cider. Let sit for 5 minutes and allow to curdle to create "buttermilk." Whisk in 1 egg and olive oil. Pour wet ingredients into dry and combine with garlic, kale, and feta. Heat a waffle maker and cook waffles according to machine directions, about 5–7 minutes per waffle. Top cooked waffles with fried egg, avocado, and salsa.

crepes two ways

Crepe Batter:
¾ cup buckwheat flour
¼ cup teff flour
¼ tsp salt
4 eggs
1 cup almond milk
2 tbsp coconut oil

In a large bowl combine dry ingredients. Add in eggs and almond milk and whisk together to combine. Heat a medium skillet or crepe pan over medium heat. Add coconut oil and heat until melted. Add crepe batter and swirl to coat the pan (about ¼ cup). Cook until edges appear to dry then flip. Set aside.

mushroom, spinach + mozzarella buckwheat + teff crepes

· ·

vegetarian, gluten-free

Filling:
1 tbsp coconut oil
1 onion
8 oz mushrooms
8 oz spinach
4 oz fresh mozzarella, sliced

In a large skillet over medium heat, add 1 tbsp coconut oil. Add onions

and cook until fragrant and browned, 5–7 minutes. Add mushrooms and continue to cook for another 7 minutes. Add spinach and mozzarella and cook until spinach is just wilted. Divide mushroom spinach filling among crepes. Fold and serve.

bananas foster buckwheat + teff crepes

· ·

vegan, gluten-free

Filling:
3 tbsp vegan butter
⅓ cup coconut sugar
4 firm bananas, peeled, cut lengthwise
⅓ cup dark rum

In a separate large sauté pan over low heat, combine coconut sugar and vegan butter. Stir until sugar dissolves. Add bananas and cook for 2–3 minutes. Add rum, and if sauce is hot enough, it will flame on its own. Otherwise, tilt pan away from you until it catches. Continue cooking until flame dies out. Divide bananas among crepes. Fold and pour remaining sauce on top.

pan-seared oatmeal
sticks with berries

vegan, gluten-free

10 oz Purely Elizabeth Ancient Grain Original Oatmeal
1½ cups almond milk
1 tbsp coconut oil
maple syrup
fresh berries

In a loaf pan, combine oats and almond milk. Stir to combine. Store in the refrigerator overnight to allow the oats to soak. In the morning, cut oatmeal into slices. Heat coconut oil in a large skillet over medium heat. Add sliced oatmeal. Sear on both sides for 3–5 minutes or until browned. Serve with maple syrup and fresh berries.

CHAPTER 11

seasonal menus to celebrate.

One of my favorite things about cooking and eating is sharing it with friends and family. I love entertaining, and there's nothing better than wowing your guests with the freshest, most delicious seasonal produce. Nothing says summer like fresh-cut sweet corn or caps off a golden day at the beach like a ripe peach bellini. A skewer of roasted Brussels sprouts and a sip of spiked apple cider take the chill out of the crisp fall air as winter moves in. I tend to live by the motto that every day is a celebration, so don't wait for that special occasion—invite some friends over and create one of these purely delicious menu combinations. Go ahead and celebrate with the people you love most. Cheers!

spring brunch

· ·

FAVA BEAN CROSTINI WITH OLIVE OIL,
PARMESAN + MINT | 51
SPICY KALE WITH STRAWBERRY, MINT,
JALAPEÑO + SHAVED PARMESAN | 89
CHIA SEED JAM THREE WAYS – GRANOLA PARFAIT STATION | 311
SPRING VEGETABLE FRITTATA | 287
RAW RASPBERRY LEMON CHEESECAKE | 209
FRESH PEACH STRAWBERRY BELLINI | 259

summer soiree

· ·

TOMATO GAZPACHO | 121
HEMP PESTO PASTA WITH TOMATOES,
ZUCCHINI + FAVA BEANS | 163
BLUEBERRY GRANOLA CRISP | 221
MAKE YOUR OWN MOJITO BAR | 268

fall harvest

....

**GRILLED POLENTA BITES WITH PISTACHIO PESTO
+ GRILLED TOMATOES** | 45

**KALE CAESAR SALAD WITH GRILLED PORTOBELLO
+ POLENTA CROUTONS** | 85

**QUINOA-CRUSTED EGGPLANT PARMESAN OVER SWISS
CHARD + WHITE BEANS** | 160

POACHED PEARS WITH COCONUT WHIPPED CREAM | 209

SPIKED APPLE CIDER MARTINI | 267

winter's bounty

....

**ROASTED GRAPES, PISTACHIO, GOAT CHEESE
+ TRUFFLE HONEY** | 37

BROCCOLI POTATO SOUP | 113

**PAN-SEARED HALIBUT WITH PESTO GNOCCHI
+ BRUSSELS SPROUTS** | 181

WARM BAKED APPLE WITH OATMEAL CRUMBLE | 242

**CHAMPAGNE, VODKA + ST. GERMAIN
WITH POMEGRANATE** | 273

Index

notes

....

....

....

....

....

....

....

....

....

....

....

....

notes

notes

notes

notes